Company's Coming

CRAFTS

Beading
Beautiful Accessories in Under an Hour

Redefined Glamour, page 94

Front Cover: Spearmint Twist, Page 128

Beading

First Printing December 2008

Library and Archives Canada Cataloguing in Publication
Beading: beautiful accessories in under an hour.
(Creative Series)
Includes index.
At head of title: Company's Coming crafts.
ISBN 978-1-897477-00-7
1. Beadwork. I. Series: Creative series (Edmonton, Alta.)
TT860.B43 2008   745.58'2   C2008-902994-1

Published by
Company's Coming Publishing Limited
2311-96 Street
Edmonton, Alberta, Canada T6N 1G3
Tel: 780-450-6223 Fax: 780-450-1857
www.companyscoming.com

THE COMPANY'S COMING STORY

Jean Paré grew up with an understanding that family, friends and home cooking are the key ingredients for a good life. A mother of four, Jean worked as a professional caterer for 18 years, operating out of her home kitchen. During that time, she came to appreciate quick and easy recipes that call for everyday ingredients. In answer to mounting requests for her recipes, Company's Coming cookbooks were born, and Jean moved on to a new chapter in her career.

In the beginning, Jean worked from a spare bedroom in her home, located in the small prairie town of Vermilion, Alberta, Canada. The first Company's Coming cookbook, *150 Delicious Squares*, was an immediate bestseller. Today, with well over 150 titles in print, Company's Coming has earned the distinction of publishing Canada's most popular cookbooks. The company continues to gain new supporters by adhering to Jean's "Golden Rule of Cooking"— Never share a recipe you wouldn't use yourself. It's an approach that has worked—millions of times over!

Company's Coming cookbooks are distributed throughout Canada, the United States, Australia and other international English-language markets. French and Spanish language editions have also been published. Sales to date have surpassed 25 million copies with no end in sight. Familiar and trusted in home kitchens around the world, Company's

Company's Coming founder Jean Paré

Coming cookbooks are highly regarded both as kitchen workbooks and as family heirlooms.

Just as Company's Coming continues to promote the tradition of home cooking, the same is now true with crafting. Like good cooking, great craft results depend upon easy-to-follow instructions, readily available materials and enticing photographs of the finished products. Also like cooking, crafting is meant to be enjoyed in the home or cottage. Company's Coming Crafts, then, is a natural extension from the kitchen into the family room or den.

Because Company's Coming operates a test kitchen and not a craft shop, we've partnered with a major North American craft content publisher to assemble a variety of craft compilations exclusively for us. Our editors have been involved every step of the way. You can see the excellent results for yourself in the book you're holding.

Company's Coming Crafts are for everyone— whether you're a beginner or a seasoned pro. What better gift could you offer than something you've made yourself? In these hectic days, people still enjoy crafting parties; they bring family and friends together in the same way a good meal does. Company's Coming is proud to support crafters with this new creative book series.

We hope you enjoy these easy-to-follow, informative and colourful books, and that they inspire your creativity! So, don't delay—get crafty!

TABLE OF CONTENTS

Between the Covers 6 • Foreword 7 • General Instructions 8

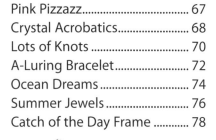

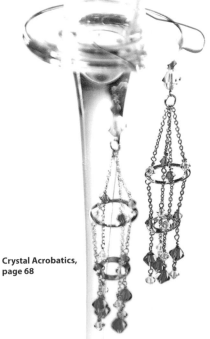

TABLE OF CONTENTS

Autumn

Create designs of rich, heart-warming colours that will make a dazzling statement.

Winter

Add a touch of sophistication to all your holiday parties and events.

**Ice Is Nice,
page 136**

**Rainforest Jasper,
page 84**

**Silver Spacers
Bracelet & Earrings,
page 140**

**Lady in Red,
page 134**

Between the Covers

Beading
Beautiful Accessories in Under an Hour
Beading has never been more popular, even though it is a centuries-old art form. Complement your wardrobe, give your home extra flair or add an extra-special personal touch to gifts with these quick and easy beading projects. From gorgeous beaded showpieces to complete jewelry sets, you can create many of these season-by-season projects in less than an hour. With *Beading* as your guide, you can craft beautiful accessories year-round—and have lots of fun doing it!

◄ Refined Glamour, page 94

Crocheting
Easy Blankets, Throws & Wraps
Whether you're a stitching expert or complete novice, *Crocheting* offers page after page of inspiration. Find projects perfect for decorating your home, for looking great while staying warm or for giving that one-of-a-kind gift. Step-by-step instructions, basic tutorials for beginners and a range of simple but stunning projects make crocheting quick, easy and entertaining. Once you start, you'll be hooked!

◄ Gramma & Grandbabies, page 60

Sewing
Fun Weekend Projects
What do you get when you take a sewing machine, a weekend and this collection of fun projects? How about a table runner, bread basket, baby blanket, sewing caddy, shoulder bag or decorative cushion? *Sewing* offers a wide assortment of easy and attractive projects to help you create practical storage solutions, decorations for any room or just the right gift for that someone special. Make it fast and make it special with great designs from *Sewing*.

◄ Pillow Trio, page 102

Also look for Company's Coming *Card Making*, *Knitting* and *Patchwork Quilting* craft books.

For more information about Company's Coming craft books, visit our website, www.companyscoming.com

FOREWORD

As you flip through the pages of our book, you'll be sure to catch the "beading bug" that is sweeping the country. There are beading shops springing up everywhere, and the large craft stores are adorning their aisles with beautiful, luscious beading components that are sure to call your name. If you are like me, you might already have quite the stash of jewellery components and are just waiting to string them into dazzling designs you'll be proud to wear.

We've included over 110 splendid designs just for you in three different skill levels from beginner to intermediate. The book is divided up into four chapters—Spring, Summer, Autumn and Winter. You'll find many stunning necklaces, dazzling bracelets, deliciously fun earrings, sophisticated watches, sparkly home decor and fun accessories. There are projects suitable for wearing with barely-there summer attire and with chunky winter sweaters, with elegant party attire and with casual jeans. For the nature enthusiast, we've even included a bracelet made from fishing lures.

With these step-by-step instructions, full-colour photography and your own creativity, it won't be long until you are making beautiful bead creations for your wardrobe. Find a design you love and decide whether you want to follow the design as is or change one of the elements—size, colour, texture, materials, theme. It can be intimidating to alter a design, but once you've been beading for a while, you'll soon be making jewellery to match every outfit you wear.

Most designs can be made—start to finish—in a half hour or so. A few will take a little more time, but you'll think they're well worth it when you start receiving compliments about your jewellery. It will make you proud to be able to say thanks for the kind words and tell your friends you made it yourself.

So, what are you waiting for? Get out your bead stash or drive to the nearest bead store where you can select stunning beading components to make one of our beautiful designs. We've also included a source listing with each set of instructions.

No matter what the season, you'll have fun beading all year through.

Copper Dreams, page 36

Spring Awakening, page 32

GENERAL INSTRUCTIONS

Techniques

Crimping

1. String the crimp tube or bead onto beading wire. Pass wire through loop of clasp and back through the crimp tube. With crimp tube in the outer oval-shaped section of crimp pliers, shape crimp into an oval.

2. Place crimp in the C-shaped section of crimp pliers, holding

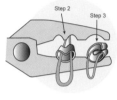

wires so that they do not cross within the crimp tube.

3. Finish by folding crimp within oval-shaped section of crimp pliers.

Wire Working

Opening Jump Rings

Open a jump ring by pushing the ends away from

each other in an up-and-down motion (not left to right) using chain-nose pliers, one set in each hand.

Simple Loop

1. With chain-nose pliers, make a 90-degree bend in the wire (A).
2. With round-nose pliers, grasp

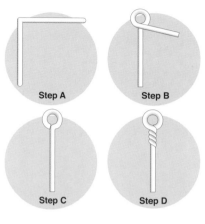

Step A Step B
Step C Step D

wire after the bend and roll wire to make a complete loop (B).
3. Trim excess wire with flush cutters (C). Open loop as you would a jump ring.

Wrapped Loop

1. Complete steps 1 and 2 of the Simple Loop. (Refer to Step B, above.)
2. Holding the loop flat between chain-nose pliers, tightly coil the tail of the wire around the neck of the wire (D). Tighten the wire with chain-nose pliers and trim excess wire with flush cutters.

Knots

Overhand Knot

Make a loop and pass the cord behind the loop, over the front cord. Pull to tighten.

Overhand Knot

Square Knot

Make one overhand knot, passing the right cord over the left. Repeat overhand knot, this time passing left end over right. Pull to tighten.

Square Knot

Surgeon's Knot

Make an overhand knot, passing the right cord over the left. Repeat overhand knot, this time passing left end over right twice. Pull to tighten.

Surgeon's Knot

Lark's Head Knot

Fold stringing material in half and pass the folded end through the loop through which you are attaching cord. Pull ends of cord through the loop made at the fold to tighten.

Lark's Head Knot

Standard Lengths

Bracelet: 6–7 inches
Choker: 15–16 inches
Princess: 18–20 inches
Matinee: 23–27 inches
Lariat: 42 inches or more

Basic Materials

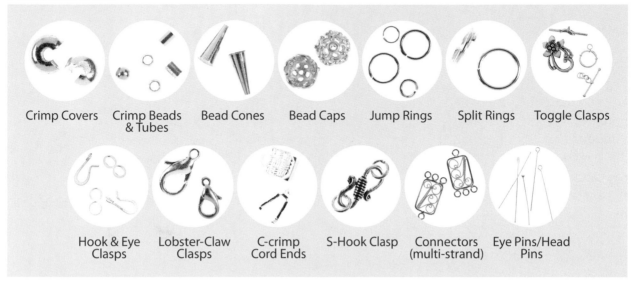

Crimp Covers   Crimp Beads & Tubes   Bead Cones   Bead Caps   Jump Rings   Split Rings   Toggle Clasps

Hook & Eye Clasps   Lobster-Claw Clasps   C-crimp Cord Ends   S-Hook Clasp   Connectors (multi-strand)   Eye Pins/Head Pins

Basic Tools

Crimp Pliers
Use these tools to crimp and fold crimp beads.

Round-Nose Pliers
The rounded jaws of these pliers are useful for creating loops on beaded head and eye pins.

Wire-Looping Pliers
A graduating round jaw creates loops in three sizes. The concave jaw gently coaxes difficult wire into loops.

Memory Wire Shears
Because memory wire is harder than beading wire or craft wire, it will damage regular wire nippers. These heavy-duty shears easily cut through memory wire and leave a clean end.

Chain-Nose Pliers
The most versatile pliers, these are useful for everything from bending eye pins to flattening crimps.

Wire Nippers
This tool is great for cutting soft wire.

Amethyst & Olivine

This classy necklace and earring set uses the season's hottest colour combination.

DESIGNS BY SANDY PARPART

Skill Level: Easy

Materials
5 (8mm) amethyst round beads
4 inches light amethyst bead chips
  (approximately 35–40)
8 (6mm) olivine bicone crystal beads
13-inch strand 11/0 purple seed beads
  (approximately 135–140)
9mm sterling silver flower with 6 loops
16 (5 x 3mm) sterling silver bead caps
10 (5mm) sterling silver daisy spacers
3 (4mm) sterling silver jump rings
3 (1½-inch) 24-gauge sterling silver head pins
2 (1½-inch) 24-gauge sterling silver eye pins
6 (1.3mm) silver crimp beads
2 sterling silver ear wires
4 x 10mm sterling silver lobster-claw clasp
26 inches .018-inch-diameter 7-strand nylon-
  coated flexible beading wire
Round-nose pliers
Needle-nose pliers
Crimp pliers
Wire nippers

Finished Sizes
Necklace
18 inches (including clasp), plus a 2½-inch dangle
Earrings
2⅛ inches long

Instructions
*Project note: Bead caps should cup the
olivine beads.*

Necklace
1. Cut beading wire into two 11-inch lengths and
one 4-inch length.
2. String a crimp bead ½ inch from one end of an
11-inch wire; thread short wire tail through clasp
and back through crimp bead. Use crimp pliers to
flatten and fold the crimp bead.
3. String 6 inches of seed beads. String a bead cap,
olivine bicone bead, bead cap, ¾ inch bead chips
and daisy spacer.
4. String an amethyst round bead. Repeat step 3,
only in reverse and do not string the seed beads.

5. String a crimp bead; thread wire through one hole of sterling silver flower and back through crimp bead and several other beads. Flatten and fold the crimp bead. Trim excess wire.

6. Repeat steps 2–5, attaching beaded wire to opposite side of flower, referring to photo for placement. Substitute jump ring in place of clasp.

7. For dangle, slide a seed bead, bead cap, olivine bicone bead, bead cap and a seed bead on a head pin; use round-nose pliers to form a wrapped head-pin loop above top bead. Trim excess wire.

8. String a crimp bead ½ inch from one end of 4-inch wire; thread short wire tail through wrapped head-pin loop and back through crimp bead. Flatten and fold the crimp bead.

9. String the following: seed bead, daisy spacer, amethyst round bead, daisy spacer, ¾ inch bead chips, bead cap, olivine bicone bead and bead cap; thread wire through bottom loop of flower and back through crimp bead. Flatten and fold the crimp bead. Trim excess wire.

Earrings

1. Repeat step 7 of necklace twice.

2. Slide the following on an eye pin: seed bead, daisy spacer, amethyst round bead, daisy spacer and a seed bead; form a loop above top bead. Trim excess wire. Repeat once.

3. Open top loops of beaded head pins and attach to bottom loops of beaded eye pins; close loops.

4. Open a jump ring and slide on top loop of eye pin; attach jump ring to ear wire. Close jump ring. Repeat for second earring. ■

SOURCE: Crimp beads and beading wire from Beadalon.

A Wing & A Prayer

Kazuri beads accent this handmade ceramic centre-piece in an avian necklace with asymmetrical appeal.

DESIGN BY MOLLY SCHALLER

Skill Level: Easy

Materials
Kazuri beads: 2 (⅞-inch) pillow, 2 (½-inch) pillow, 1 (⅜-inch) round
¾-inch wooden pillow bead
12 molten silver beads
10 (4mm) turquoise round beads
15/0 seed beads: 2 inches plus 3 red, 2 inches green, 2 inches brown
Bird on a branch pendant
2 (5mm) jump rings
2-inch silver eye pin
2 Scrimp findings
12mm toggle clasp
9¾ inches chain with links
3 (9-inch) lengths .018-inch-diameter 19-strand nylon-coated flexible beading wire
Scrimp screwdriver
Round-nose pliers
Chain-nose pliers
Flush cutters

Finished Size
19 inches (including clasp)

Instructions
1. Cut chain into the following lengths: 4¼ inches, 4¾ inches and ¾ inch.
2. Onto the eye pin, slide one turquoise round, one ⅞-inch pillow Kazuri bead and one turquoise round.
3. Use round-nose pliers to form a loop after last bead; trim excess wire.

4. Use a jump ring to attach one half of toggle clasp to 4¾-inch piece of chain. Onto opposite end of chain, attach eye pin link. Attach ¾-inch length of chain to opposite end of link.
5. Holding the three beading wires as one, string one Scrimp finding ½ inch onto wires. Pass wires through ¾-inch link and back through the Scrimp finding. Tighten the Scrimp finding.
6. Still holding all three wires as one, string the following: one turquoise round, two molten silver beads, ½-inch pillow Kazuri bead, two molten silver beads and one turquoise round.
7. Separate wires. Onto each wire, string 2 inches of seed beads.
8. Holding wires as one, string the pendant and the following: one turquoise round, round Kazuri bead, one turquoise round, two molten silver beads, ⅞-inch pillow Kazuri bead, two molten silver beads, one turquoise round, ½-inch pillow Kazuri bead and one turquoise round.
9. Separate wires and string one red seed bead onto each one.
10. Holding wires as one, string the following: one turquoise round, two molten silver beads, wooden pillow bead, two molten silver beads, one turquoise round and Scrimp finding.
11. Pass wires through 4¼-inch chain link and back through the Scrimp. Pass wires back through beads. Tighten the Scrimp and trim excess wire.
12. Attach other end of toggle clasp to opposite end of chain with second jump ring. ∎

SOURCES: Beading wire and Scrimp findings from Beadalon; wooden bead from Westrim Crafts; Kazuri beads from Kazuri Beads USA; pendant from Diane Hawkey; chain from Thunderbird Supply Co.; toggle clasp from SHIANA; turquoise beads, molten silver beads and seed beads from Fire Mountain Gems and Beads.

Iced Key

This monochromatic, light-as-a-whisper design will dance across your neck and dazzle your senses.

DESIGN BY MARGOT POTTER

Skill Level: Intermediate

Materials
5 (12mm) cream Swarovski crystal pearls
10 (9 x 12mm) Swarovski crystal AB faceted oval beads
6 (7mm) cream faceted freshwater pearls
6 (4mm) Swarovski crystal AB top-drilled flowers
16 (6mm) cream freshwater petal pearls
6mm vintage rose Swarovski crystal rondelle bead
⁹⁄₁₆-inch Swarovski crystal scalloped-edge pendant
Small silver metal key charm
20-gauge sterling silver head pin
7mm sterling silver jump ring
2 (1.5mm) silver crimp tubes
½-inch sterling silver lobster-claw clasp
2 inches silver-plated medium curb chain
3 (20-inch) lengths .018-inch-diameter silver-plated nylon-coated flexible beading wire
2 pairs chain-nose pliers
Large crimp tool
Flush cutters

Finished Size
15 inches (including clasp), with a 2-inch extender

Instructions
1. Hold all three wires together and string a crimp tube ½ inch from one end; place wire ends through clasp and back through crimp tube, making sure to keep wire uncrossed inside tube prior to crimping. Use crimp pliers to flatten and fold the crimp tube. Trim excess wires on short ends only.
2. String a crystal flower on one wire, a faceted pearl on second wire and a petal pearl on third wire; smooth wires with fingers to separate them slightly and keep them uncrossed. Hold wires together and string a faceted oval bead.
3. Determine centre wire and string a 12mm crystal pearl. String a petal pearl on each outside wire. Smooth wires with fingers again to separate; hold wires together and string a faceted oval bead.
4. Repeat steps 2 and 3 four additional times.
5. Repeat step 2, only string a crimp tube in place of faceted oval bead.
6. Thread wire ends through a jump ring and back through crimp tube in the same manner as before. Flatten and fold the crimp tube. Trim excess wires.
7. Open jump ring and attach to end link of 2-inch chain; close ring.
8. Slide the vintage rose rondelle on a head pin; use round-nose pliers to form a wrapped head-pin loop above rondelle. Trim excess wire.
9. Open end link of chain and slide on head pin, key charm and crystal pendant; close link. ■

SOURCES: Crystal pearls, crystal beads, crystal flowers and pendant from Swarovski North America; freshwater petal pearls from WonderSources Inc.; key charm from Sacred Kitsch Studio; beading wire, chain and findings from Beadalon.

Disc-O Combo

Solid aluminum washers with wire, chains and crystals create a necklace that will turn heads.

DESIGNS BY LAURIE D'AMBROSIO

Skill Level: Easy

Materials
3 (1¼-inch) solid aluminum washers
11 (16 x 6mm) olivine green glass discs
Peridot Swarovski crystal beads: 12 (4mm)
    cube, 10 (6mm) bicone
Silver lobster-claw clasp
Silver-plated medium link chain
102 inches 20-gauge silver-coloured
    copper wire
Round-nose pliers
Chain-nose pliers
Wire cutters

Finished Sizes
Long Necklace
35½ inches with a 6-inch pendant
Short Necklace
19¼ inches (including clasp)

Instructions
Long Necklace
Centre Droplet
1. Cut one piece of chain that measures 19 links long and another piece that measures 29 links long. Cut one 6-inch length of wire.
2. Form a wrapped loop ½ inch from one end of wire, attaching chains to loop before wrapping. When attaching chains, slide on the end link of the short chain and the 17th link on the long chain. This will give the illusion that there are three pieces of chain instead of two.

3. String a peridot cube, olivine green glass disc and a peridot cube. Wrap wire tail onto an aluminum washer and proceed to wrap wire around itself at base of washer, securing wire to washer. Trim excess wire.

Chain

1. Cut eight pieces of chain, each measuring 15 links long. Cut eleven 6-inch lengths of wire.

2. In the same manner as in step 3 of centre droplet, attach a wire to opposite side of the original aluminum washer. Form a wrapped loop at opposite end, attaching loop to a chain before wrapping. Trim excess wire.

3. Form a wrapped loop with another wire, attaching loop to end link on previous chain before wrapping. String a peridot cube, olivine green glass disc and a peridot cube. Form a wrapped loop, attaching loop to another chain before wrapping. Trim excess wire.

4. Form a wrapped loop at one end of another wire, attaching loop to end link of previous chain before wrapping. Proceed to wrap wire on an aluminum washer in the same manner as before. Trim excess wire.

5. Attach another piece of wire to opposite side of the previous aluminum washer and form a wrapped loop with wire tail, attaching loop to a chain before wrapping.

6. Repeat step 3 three times.

7. Repeat steps 4 and 5. Repeat step 3. Form a wrapped loop at one end of remaining wire, attaching loop to end link of previous chain before wrapping. Proceed to wrap wire on original aluminum washer. Trim excess wire.

Short Necklace

1. Cut four pieces of chain, each measuring 14 links long. Cut five 6-inch lengths of wire.

2. Form a wrapped loop ½ inch from one end of one wire, attaching loop to clasp before wrapping. String a peridot bicone bead, olivine green glass disc and a peridot bicone. Form a wrapped loop, attaching loop to end link on a piece of chain before wrapping. Trim excess wire.

3. Repeat step 2, only attach first loop to end link of previous chain before wrapping. Continue in the same manner to attach remaining chains and wires. ■

SOURCES: Olivine green glass discs from Halcraft USA; Swarovski crystals from Pure Allure; chain from Blue Moon Beads; copper wire from NSI Innovations.

Dazzling Dragonflies

Two silver dragonflies flit across your neck, dancing on a pool of pearls and flashing crystals. Elegant and enchanting, this design is sure to become a favourite.

DESIGN BY CAITO AMOROSE

Skill Level: Easy

Materials

35 (6–6.5mm) white freshwater rice pearls
34 (4mm) AB Swarovski crystal bicone beads
66 (4mm) sterling silver jump rings
2 (6mm) sterling silver split rings
Pewter dragonfly clasp
11½ feet (138 inches) 24-gauge sterling silver wire
Round-nose pliers
Chain-nose pliers
Wire nippers

Finished Size

14½ inches (including clasp)

Instructions

1. Cut 69 lengths of sterling silver wire, each measuring 2 inches.
2. Use round-nose pliers to form a wrapped loop ½ inch from one end of a 2-inch wire. Slide a freshwater pearl onto wire and create another wrapped loop. Trim excess wire. Repeat for each freshwater pearl.
3. Repeat step 2 for each of the bicone beads.
4. Open a jump ring with chain-nose pliers and slide on a pearl link and a bicone bead link; close jump ring.
5. In the same manner, continue using jump rings to connect links together until a chain consisting of 11 pearl links and 10 bicone bead links has been formed. This will be one chain.
6. In the same manner, create a second chain consisting of 12 bicone bead links and 11 pearl links.
7. In the same manner, create a third chain consisting of 13 pearl links and 12 bicone bead links.
8. Attach one end of each chain, in order of length, to a split ring. Attach one half of clasp to split ring. Repeat on other end of necklace. ■

SOURCE: Pearls, beads and clasp from Fire Mountain Gems and Beads.

The Language of Flowers

Dried rosebuds from a special occasion make a romantic statement as earring embellishments.

DESIGN BY CAITO AMOROSE

Skill Level: Easy

Materials

2 (⅝-inch) dried rosebuds
2 (5mm) pink freshwater pearls
2 (4mm) Colorado topaz Swarovski crystal
   bicone beads
2 (1½-inch) gold eye pins
2 (1-inch) gold head pins
2 gold French ear wires
Embroidery needle
Round-nose pliers
Chain-nose pliers
Wire nippers

Finished Size

2 inches long

Instructions

1. Snip off any hard stems from rosebuds.

2. Position the rosebud so that the top of the rose is pointing downward. Pierce the bud from top to bottom with the embroidery needle to allow for an easy centring guide when sliding the eye pin through.

3. Slide a rosebud and a bicone crystal on an eye pin. Use round-nose pliers to form a wrapped loop above crystal. Trim excess wire. Repeat once.

4. Slide a pearl on a head pin; form a wrapped head-pin loop above pearl. Trim excess wire. Repeat once.

5. Open bottom loops of eye pins and slide on pearl head pins; close loops. Open ear-wire loops and attach to top loops of eye pins; close loops. ■

SOURCE: Freshwater pearls, Swarovski crystals and findings from Fire Mountain Gems and Beads.

Dragonflies

Piece together some fun puzzle earrings.

DESIGN BY MICHELLE MACH

Skill Level: Easy

Materials

4 (8/0) silver-lined green seed beads
2 (6mm) olivine Swarovski crystal bicone beads
2 (14 x 14mm) sterling silver dragonfly charms
2 sterling silver dragonfly puzzle-piece connectors

2 silver ear wires
2 (2-inch) lengths 21-gauge silver wire
Round-nose pliers
Chain-nose pliers
Wire nippers

Finished Size

2⅝ inches long

Instructions

1. Use round-nose pliers to form a small loop at one end of a 2-inch wire; open loop and slide on dragonfly charm. Close loop.

2. Slide a green seed bead, olivine bicone bead and a green seed bead on wire; form a loop above top bead. Trim excess wire.

3. Open loop and slide on puzzle piece; close loop. Open loop on ear wire and slide on opposite side of puzzle piece; close loop.

4. Repeat steps 1–3 for second earring, making sure to flip puzzle piece over to show reverse side. ■

SOURCES: Puzzle-piece connectors from Penny Michelle; crystals, dragonfly charms and wire from Fire Mountain Gems and Beads; seed beads and ear wires from The Bead Cache Inc.

Dragonfly Fun

Make dragonfly zipper pulls, necklace charms, and earrings in a variety of ways. Kids will love personalizing them by using their friends' favourite colours or initials.

DESIGNS BY DEBBIE TUTTLE

Skill Level: Beginner

Materials

Crystal bicone beads: 2 (3mm) light pink,
   2 (4mm) yellow, 2 (4mm) peach, 2 (4mm)
   olive green, 2 (4mm) clear, 2 (5mm) pink,
   2 (6mm) turquoise (for earrings)
Assorted 4–7mm beads (for zipper pulls)
Additional 4mm crystal bicone beads in various
   colours (for bookmark)
4.5mm sterling silver alphabet blocks to spell
   desired word or name
Hematite heart-shaped beads:
   2 (5mm), 2 (6mm)
7 silver dragonfly wings
3 silver zipper pulls
7 (2-inch) silver head pins
6mm silver split ring
5 silver jump rings
2 silver ball-and-post earring findings
18-inch silver chain with attached clasp
Ribbon bookmark
Round-nose pliers
Chain-nose pliers
Wire nippers

Finished Sizes

Necklace
18 inches (including clasp)

Earrings
1½ inches long
Zipper Pulls
2¼ inches long
Bookmark
15 inches long

Instructions

1. Slide three to six beads onto a 2-inch head pin, starting with the smallest bead first. Follow these with a dragonfly wings bead and one more bead.
2. Use round-nose pliers to form a loop above top bead. Trim excess wire.
3. Open a jump ring or split ring and attach to beaded head pin; close ring. (Omit ring if making earrings. Attach head pin loop directly to earring posts.)
4. Slide ring onto chain, ribbon or zipper pull. ■

SOURCES: Dragonfly wings from Eclectic Etc. Inc.; crystal beads from Swarovski North America; alphabet blocks from Accents Beads; beads, split ring, chain and ear posts from Rio Grande.

Cellphone Savvy

Ring! Ring! Do you know where your cellphone is? These fabulous accessories will help you keep track of your phone.

DESIGNS BY CANDIE COOPER

Wristlet

Skill Level: Beginner

Materials
4mm fire opal Swarovski bicone bead
8 x 10mm green leaf bead
10mm red flower bead
6mm orange glass pearl
6mm silver leaf bead cap
Silver butterfly charm
Jump rings: 1 (5mm), 1 (8mm)
Cellphone strap
2-inch silver head pin
2-inch silver eye pin
13mm silver clamp end
10 inches ½-inch-wide decorative ribbon
Round-nose pliers
Flat-nose pliers
Wire nippers

Finished Size
7 inches long

Instructions
1. Fold ribbon in half; place ribbon ends inside a clamp end and use flat-nose pliers to secure clamp in place.
2. Open loop on eye pin and slide on butterfly charm; close loop. String a pearl and a leaf bead cap; form a wrapped loop above bead cap. Trim excess wire. Open 5mm jump ring and attach to loop; close ring.
3. Slide a leaf bead, fire opal bicone and a flower bead on a head pin; form a wrapped loop above top bead. Trim excess wire.
4. Open the 8mm jump ring and slide on butterfly dangle, cellphone strap and 3mm jump ring; attach ring to crimp end. Close jump ring.

CONTINUED ON PAGE 26

Beaded Chain

Skill Level: Beginner

Materials
Silver fish beads: 1 (35 x 24mm), 1 (15 x 10mm)
Swarovski crystal bicone beads: 12 (4mm)
    aquamarine, 2 (6mm) light Colorado topaz
16 (4mm) copper Swarovski crystal round beads
10 (8 x 6mm) aqua oval glass beads
20 (5mm) silver spacers
4 aquamarine small star double-hole slider beads
5 (12mm) white coin pearls
Porcelain charms: 1 starfish, 1 shell
38mm silver swivel badge clip
2 silver Wire Guardians
2 (4.5mm) silver round Scrimp findings
Blue cellphone strap
5 (12mm) aquamarine crystal links
Jump rings: 1 (8mm), 3 (5mm)
2 (2-inch) silver head pins
2 (6-inch) lengths 18-gauge silver wire
15 inches .018-inch-diameter 49-strand
    nylon-coated flexible beading wire
Round-nose pliers
Chain-nose pliers
Wire nippers
Mini screwdriver

Finished Size
19¾ inches (including clip)

Instructions
1. Form a wrapped loop at one end of a 6-inch piece of 18-gauge wire, attaching loop to badge clip before wrapping. Trim excess wire. String a copper round, 35 x 24mm fish bead and a copper round. Form a wrapped loop, attaching loop to an aquamarine crystal link before wrapping. Trim excess wire.
2. Repeat step 1, using the 15 x 10mm fish bead and connecting it to the crystal link below the large fish.
3. String a Scrimp finding and Wire Guardian 1 inch from one end of beading wire; insert short wire tail through previous crystal link and back through the

Scrimp finding. Position the Scrimp finding next to the Wire Guardian and tighten the screw.
4. String a copper round, silver spacer, aqua oval, silver spacer, aquamarine bicone, coin pearl, aquamarine bicone, silver spacer, aqua oval, silver spacer, copper round and a slider bead. Repeat four additional times, but do not string the last slider bead.
5. String a Scrimp finding and a Wire Guardian; pass wire through an aquamarine crystal link and back through Scrimp finding and copper round. Gently pull wire taut and tighten screw to secure Scrimp. Trim excess wire.
6. Slide a light Colorado topaz bicone, aquamarine bicone and a copper round on a head pin. Form a wrapped loop above beads; trim excess wire. Repeat once.
7. Open a 5mm jump ring and slide on starfish charm and an aquamarine crystal link; close ring. Repeat with shell charm.
8. Use 5mm jump rings to connect a beaded dangle from step 6 and shell charm dangle to swivel clip. Open the 8mm jump ring and slide on starfish charm dangle, crystal dangle from step 6, cellphone strap and beaded chain. Close jump ring.

Pouch

Skill Level: Beginner

Materials
3 aqua E beads
10mm purple cubic zirconia charm
15–20 assorted beads
Silver elephant charm
3 (2-inch) gold eye pins
2-inch gold head pin
2 (12mm) eye findings (from hook-and-eye set)
Gold jump rings: 1 (12mm), 3 (6mm)
16.8mm gold toggle clasp
6 inches brown polyester chain
Orange embroidered felt
22mm blue mirror appliqué embellishment
2-inch green tassel
6 inches ½-inch-wide white/orange polka-dot
    ribbon
6 inches green rickrack
Orange thread
Sewing needle
Sewing pins
Round-nose pliers
Flat-nose pliers
Crimp pliers
Wire nippers
Iron
Sewing machine (optional)
Fabric glue

Finished Size
2⅛ x 3¾ x ½ inches

Instructions
Project note: Felt measurements may need to be adjusted slightly if cellphone is larger than sample used.

1. Cut a 2¾ x 7¾-inch piece of felt. Fold felt in half right sides facing; machine- or hand-stitch right and left sides using a ¼-inch seam allowance.

2. Turn piece right side out and press flat with an iron. Check fit of phone; if it is a little snug, trim a little of the inside seam.

3. Thread needle and anchor three stitches near top inside left edge of the pouch over the seam. Slide the next-to-last link of the polyester chain onto the eye finding; secure eye finding to inside of the pouch with several stitches. Anchor thread in the same manner as before. Repeat on opposite side.

4. Beginning on back of pouch, glue ribbon to top edge; leave a ½-inch tail. *Note: Use pins to hold ribbon in place while it dries.* Repeat to glue rickrack on top of the ribbon. Turn under ½-inch tails and secure with a few hand stitches.

5. Glue mirror embellishment to front of pouch as shown; let dry. For additional security, add a few stitches along edges of embellishment. Hand-stitch tassel to pouch just below embellishment.

6. String assorted beads on head and eye pins. Form a loop above beads to secure each pin; trim excess wire.

7. Open loop on head pin and attach to an eye pin; close loop. Open loop on different eye pin and slide on charm; close loop. Open 12mm jump ring and slide on the following: E bead, charm dangle, E bead, head pin dangle and an E bead. Attach jump ring to last link on left side of pouch.

8. Use needle and thread to hand-stitch the cubic zirconia charm to loop on remaining eye pin; tie thread ends together in a knot. Trim excess thread. Add a dot of glue to knot; let dry. Use a 6mm jump ring to attach beaded eye pin to last link on right side of pouch.

9. Count up five chain links on right side of pouch and cut the fifth link, removing it all together. Use a 6mm jump ring to attach bar end of toggle clasp to short side of chain; repeat to attach round half of clasp to long side of chain. ∎

SOURCES: Clamp end from Rings & Things; beading wire, badge clip, polyester chain, toggle clasp, head pins, eye pins, cubic zirconia charm, Wire Guardians and Scrimp findings from Beadalon; porcelain charms from Earthenwood Studio; crystal links and star slider beads from Pure Allure; crystals from Swarovski North America; embroidered felt from Ornamentea; mirror embellishment from Wrights; tassel from Fire Mountain Gems and Beads.

Timely Reflections

Hang this mirror by the back door. Not only will it garner compliments, but you'll never be late due to last-minute preening again!

DESIGN BY MOLLY SCHALLER

Skill Level: Easy

Materials

8 x 10-inch oval mirror with predrilled holes for hanging
Gold Asian-motif watch face
3 (22 x 18mm) diamond-shaped cloisonné beads
4 (6mm) gold filigree round beads
33 (2mm) gold round beads
Swarovski crystal beads: 6 (6mm) gold AB round, 34 (4mm) blue bicone
2-inch gold eye pin
5 (1½-inch) .028-gauge gold-plated clear AB crystal-tipped head pins
2 (5mm) 18-gauge gold jump rings
6 (1.3mm) gold crimp tubes
16 inches .024-inch-diameter 49-strand nylon-coated flexible beading wire
Round-nose pliers
Flat-nose pliers
Crimp pliers
Wire nippers

Instructions

1. Slide three blue bicone crystals onto a head pin; use round-nose pliers to form a wrapped head-pin loop above top bead. Trim excess wire.
2. Repeat step 1, substituting a gold AB round crystal in place of bicone crystals. Repeat step 1, substituting a blue bicone crystal and a gold AB round crystal in place of three bicone crystals. Repeat step 1, substituting two blue bicone crystals in place of three bicone crystals. Repeat step 1, substituting a gold AB round crystal and a blue bicone crystal in place of three bicone crystals. Set aside beaded head pins.
3. Slide the following onto the eye pin: blue bicone crystal, diamond cloisonné bead and a blue bicone crystal. Form a loop above top crystal. Trim excess wire. Open bottom loop and slide on three beaded head pins; close loop.
4. Attach jump rings to top and bottom loops on watch face. Open bottom jump ring and slide on two beaded head pins; close ring.
5. String a crimp tube onto beading wire ½ inch from one end; place wire end through the bottom jump ring attached to watch face and back through crimp bead. Use crimp pliers to flatten and fold the crimp tube.
6. String a blue bicone crystal and a 2mm gold round bead; repeat four additional times. String two crimp tubes. Position the first crimp tube next to the last 2mm gold round bead and flatten it with crimp pliers, securing beads in place.
7. Position the second crimp tube approximately 1½ inches from first crimp tube; crimp and flatten it, securing it in place. **Note:** *This measurement may need to be changed slightly depending on the distance between the holes in the mirror. The exposed wire should not show when mirror is hung.*
8. Thread wire end through the right hole in the mirror so wire is on front. String two 2mm gold round beads, gold filigree bead, diamond

CONTINUED ON PAGE 45

Snappy Cuff Watch

You needn't be savvy with a sewing machine to make this snappy cuff.

DESIGN BY CANDIE COOPER

Skill Level: Easy

Materials
Swarovski crystal bicone beads: 4 (6mm) light
   rose, 2 (6mm) light peach, 4 (4mm) light peach
Silver pink-hued watch face
44 pink seed beads
1¼ x 8-inch piece each grey and gold wool felt
1¼ x 8-inch denim
½-inch snap kit
6 (2-inch) silver head pins
2 (8mm) silver jump rings
6½ inches ½-inch-wide pink floral printed ribbon
Thread: pink, burgundy
Straight pins
Sewing needle
Iron
Sewing machine
Round-nose pliers
Wire nippers
Seam sealant (optional)

Finished Size
8 inches

Instructions
1. Pin wool felt and denim pieces together back
to back with gold felt in centre. With grey felt side
faceup, machine-stitch along length
¼ inch from right edge using burgundy thread.
Machine-stitch along length again ¼ inch from first
stitched line. Continue until there are a total of four
stitched lines. Round corners of stitched piece with
scissors, being careful to not cut threads.
2. Turn ends of ribbon under ¼ inch; press with

an iron to keep ends in place. Centre ribbon on
felt side of cuff; pin ribbon in place. Use pink
thread to machine-stitch along edges of ribbon.
3. Follow manufacturer's instructions to attach
snaps to ends of cuff, making sure they are
positioned correctly.
4. Thread needle with pink thread. Centre watch
face on cuff and hand-stitch in place, securing
top and bottom of watch face. Anchor thread
in place by taking two forward stitches and one
backstitch.
5. Beginning ⅞ inch from bottom of cuff, hand-
stitch seed beads along length of first burgundy
stitched line, spacing beads approximately ½
inch apart. Continue along entire length of first
stitched line, top edge and along entire length
of last stitched line. Secure thread on back of
cuff. Trim excess thread.
6. Attach jump rings to top and bottom loops of
watch face.
7. Slide a 4mm light peach bicone bead, pink
seed bead and a light rose bicone bead on a
head pin; use round-nose pliers to form a loop
above top bead. Trim excess wire. Repeat three
additional times.
8. Slide a 6mm light peach bicone bead and two
pink seed beads on a head pin; form a loop above
top bead and trim excess wire. Repeat once.
9. Open loops on beaded head pins. Attach
head pins to jump rings at top and bottom of
watch face so there are two light rose/light
peach head pins and one light peach head pin
on each jump ring. Light peach head pins should
be in the middle. ■

SOURCE: Watch face and Swarovski crystal beads from Pure Allure.

Spring Awakening

With the advent of spring comes longer days, warm weather and flowers blooming, even on watchbands.

DESIGN BY MARY BLOOMSBURG

Skill Level: Intermediate

Materials
Swarovski crystal bicone beads: 24 (4mm) fire opal, 4 (6mm) hyacinth
2-hole crystal spacers:
   2 (12mm) topaz/rose flowers, 4 (14mm) light sapphire/hyacinth crescents
13mm crystal watch face (clasp included)
4 (2 x 2mm) sterling silver crimp beads
2 (18-inch) lengths .012-inch-diameter 19-strand nylon-coated flexible beading wire
Crimp pliers
Wire nippers

Finished Size
7 inches (including clasp)

Instructions
1. Thread one length of wire through top holes of watch face, centering wire.
2. String a fire opal bicone bead on each wire. Insert wires through a crescent spacer.
3. String a fire opal bicone bead on each wire. String a hyacinth bicone bead on one wire; insert the other wire through the same hyacinth bicone, threading wire through from the opposite direction (Fig. 1). String a fire opal bicone bead on each wire (Fig. 2).
4. Insert wires through a flower spacer. Repeat step 3. Insert wires through a crescent spacer. String a fire opal bicone bead on each wire.
5. String a crimp bead on one wire; insert wire through one hole on one half of watch clasp and back through crimp bead and last fire opal bead. Use crimp pliers to flatten and fold the crimp bead. Trim excess wire. Repeat to attach other wire to other hole on clasp.
6. Repeat steps 1–5 on other side of watch face. ■

SOURCES: Swarovski crystal beads and crimp beads from Astral Beads; watch face and crystal spacers from Bead Time Inc.; beading wire from Beadalon.

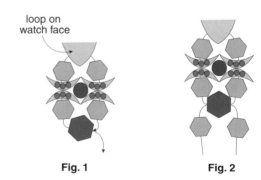

loop on watch face

Fig. 1   **Fig. 2**

Creative Curves

Gentle curves and lots of dazzle add beauty and romance to your special day. Crystal colours can easily be coordinated to match anyone's gown!

DESIGN BY CAITO AMOROSE

Skill Level: Intermediate

Materials
18 (5mm) clear Swarovski crystal bicone beads
20 (7mm) clear Swarovski crystal chaton bead caps
9 (3mm) clear Swarovski crystal rhinestone dangles
9 silver curved tube beads
2 (2 x 2mm) sterling silver crimp tubes
2 (3mm) sterling silver crimp covers
7mm sterling silver ring
7mm sterling silver spring-ring clasp
2 (9-inch) lengths .012-inch-diameter nylon-coated
    flexible beading wire
Chain-nose pliers
Crimp pliers
Wire nippers

Finished Size
7¼ inches (including clasp)

Instructions
1. Hold both wire lengths together and string on a crimp tube ½ inch from one end; place wire tail through clasp and back through crimp tube. Use crimp pliers to flatten and fold the crimp tube. Use chain-nose pliers to secure crimp cover on top of crimp tube.

2. With wires together, string two bead caps, wide opening to wide opening, positioning them so they fit snugly against each other, forming the look of a round bead.

3. Separate wires. String a curved tube bead on one strand; string a clear bicone bead, rhinestone dangle and a clear bicone bead on second strand.

4. Repeat steps 2 and 3 eight additional times. Repeat step 2.

5. With wires together, string on a crimp tube; place wire end through silver ring and back through crimp tube and a few other beads. Flatten and fold the crimp tube. Trim excess wire. Attach crimp cover on top of crimp tube. ■

SOURCES: Swarovski bicone beads, crimp tubes, crimp covers, ring, clasp and beading wire from Fire Mountain Gems & Beads; curved tube beads from Beadalon; Swarovski dangles from Swarovski North America; Swarovski bead caps from Jewelry Supply Inc.

Copper Dreams

Copper is accented with sea blue crystals in this stunning woven bracelet.

DESIGN BY MARGOT POTTER

Skill Level: Intermediate

Materials

13 (6mm) crystal copper Swarovski crystal round beads
6mm Swarovski crystal rondelles: 6 crystal golden shadow, 9 Pacific opal, 2 crystal copper
4 copper open heart charms
6 (5mm) copper jump rings
2 copper crimp covers
2 (1.3mm) copper crimp tubes
Copper lobster-claw clasp
6½ inches 20-gauge copper craft wire
2 (10-inch) lengths copper .018-inch-diameter 7-strand nylon-coated flexible beading wire
Round-nose pliers
2 pairs chain-nose pliers
Nylon-jaw pliers
Crimp pliers
Jumbo crimp pliers
Flush cutters

Finished Size

7 inches (including clasp), plus a 1-inch extender chain

Instructions

1. For coil charm, cut a 2½-inch length of 20-gauge wire. Referring to Fig. 1, use round-nose pliers to form a small loop at one end of wire; use thumb and forefinger to compress the wire, wrapping it into a coil. Use nylon-jaw pliers to keep wire flat while

Fig. 1

continuing to form the coil. Stop wrapping wire when there is ¼ inch left. Bend wire upward at a 90-degree angle from top of coil. Form a small loop at wire end. Use chain-nose pliers to bend loop so it can be threaded side to side with a jump ring. Set aside.

2. Form a small loop at one end of a 1-inch length of 20-gauge wire. String a Pacific opal rondelle and use round-nose pliers to form a wrapped loop above rondelle. Trim excess wire. Repeat three times, once with a Pacific opal rondelle and twice with crystal copper rondelles. Set aside.

3. Hold both lengths of beading wire together and string a crimp tube ½ inch from end; insert wire ends through jump ring and back through crimp tube, keeping wires uncrossed inside tube and using chain-nose pliers to pull wires through tube, making sure to not pull too tight. Use crimp pliers to flatten and fold the crimp tube.

4. Attach a crimp cover over crimp tube, using jumbo crimp tool to fold cover over into a smooth bead.

5. With wires together, string a Pacific opal rondelle. String a crystal copper round on only the right wire. Thread both wires through a crystal golden shadow rondelle. String a crystal copper round on only the left wire.

6. Repeat step 5 five times. Thread both wires through a Pacific opal rondelle. String a copper crystal rondelle on only the right wire.

7. Thread both wires through a crimp tube; insert wires through clasp and back through crimp tube.

CONTINUED ON PAGE 44

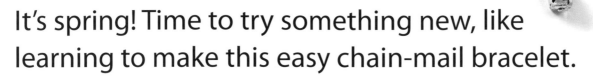

Effervescence

It's spring! Time to try something new, like learning to make this easy chain-mail bracelet.

DESIGNS BY JEAN YATES

Skill Level: Easy

Materials
13mm white gold-lined Venetian glass cubes:
    4 ruby, 4 lime, 4 clear
4 (27mm) sterling silver closed linkable rings
24 sterling silver bead caps
18-gauge sterling silver jump rings: 63 (5mm),
    44 (4mm)
Sterling silver snap-close jump rings: 6 (8mm),
    6 (6mm), 2 (4mm)
12 (22-gauge) sterling silver head pins
2 sterling silver ear wires
Sterling silver toggle clasp
Beading tray (optional)
2 pairs chain-nose pliers
Round-nose pliers
Wire nippers

Finished Sizes
Bracelet
7⅜ inches (including clasp)
Earrings
4 inches long

Project note: *If desired, use beading tray to keep jump rings organized while working.*

Instructions
Bracelet
1. Use chain-nose pliers to open 42 (18-gauge) 5mm jump rings; close the remaining 18-gauge 5mm jump rings.
2. Slide one open ring through a closed ring;

close ring. With chain-nose pliers in dominant hand, pick up a third open ring and hook it through the other, attached rings. Close ring. Lay the joined rings on tray or worktable in a swirling flower shape, making sure they remain in that shape (refer to image).

3. Repeat step 2 with remaining jump rings from step 1 to make a total of 21 "flowers."
4. Use chain-nose pliers to open all 18-gauge 4mm jump rings.
5. Slide two 4mm jump rings onto a "flower"; close rings. In the same manner, use two 4mm jump rings to attach all "flowers," creating bracelet chain.
6. Use two 4mm jump rings to attach one half of clasp to each bracelet end.
7. Slide a bead cap, cube bead and a bead cap onto a head pin, positioning bead caps so they cup the cube. Use round-nose pliers to form a wrapped head-pin loop above bead cap; trim excess wire.
8. Repeat step 7 for each cube bead. Set aside the following head pins to be used for earrings: 2 lime, 2 clear and 2 ruby.
9. Attach an 8mm snap-close jump ring to each beaded head pin. Referring to photo, attach head pins to bracelet as desired.

Earrings
1. Attach 4mm snap-close jump rings to ear wires.
2. Open a 6mm snap-close jump ring and slide it through 4mm jump ring attached to an ear wire; slide 6mm ring through a linkable ring and a lime cube head pin. Close ring.

CONTINUED ON PAGE 44

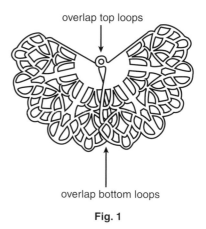

Filigree Butterfly

This butterfly beauty is perfect for tea in the garden.

DESIGNS BY TERRY RICIOLI

Skill Level: Easy

Materials

17 (11mm) pink Czech pressed glass oval beads
Pink flower cloisonné round beads: 11 (6mm), 8 (8mm)
Gold filigree round beads: 19 (3mm), 16 (5mm)
8mm gold filigree tube bead
2 (35mm) gold filigree fans
3 (2-inch) gold head pins
4 (1.3mm) gold crimp beads
2 gold Euro ear wires
Gold filigree fish clasp
8 inches 26-gauge gold wire
2 (12-inch) lengths .012-inch-diameter 7-strand nylon-coated flexible beading wire
Round-nose pliers
Crimp pliers
Wire nippers

Finished Sizes
Necklace
18¾ inches (including clasp)
Earrings
1⅜ inches long

Instructions
Necklace
1. For butterfly body, first slide the following on a head pin: 6mm cloisonné bead, pink oval, gold

filigree tube and a 3mm gold filigree round. Form a loop after last bead; trim excess wire.

2. Referring to Fig. 1, overlap top and bottom loops of filigree fans. These will be the butterfly wings. Insert both ends of 26-gauge wire through top loops front to back; pull wire ends, forming a wire loop on front of fans. Place beaded head pin through loop, positioning the wire loop between the cloisonné and pink oval bead. The cloisonné bead should be at top. Pull on wire ends to tighten wire so wire is hidden between beads.

overlap top loops

overlap bottom loops

Fig. 1

3. With wire ends on back of wings, insert wire ends through bottom loops; cross wire ends over beaded head pin between the filigree tube and filigree round and then back through bottom loops as before. Wires should be hidden between

CONTINUED ON PAGE 45

Nesting Instincts

If imitation is the sincerest form of flattery, Mother Nature will be thrilled by this charming set featuring delicate pearls nestled in a bed of antiqued silver wire.

DESIGNS BY KAREN GALBRAITH

Skill Level: Intermediate

Materials
14 (5mm) white potato pearls
20-gauge sterling silver wire, dead soft: 2 (4-inch) lengths, 1 (5-inch) length
26-gauge sterling silver, dead soft: 2 (36-inch) lengths, 1 (60-inch) length
2 sterling silver ear wires
16-inch sterling silver necklace chain with clasp
Hard-boiled egg (optional)
Small plastic container with lid (optional)
Silver jewellery polishing cloth (optional)
Wooden dowel rods: ½-inch-diameter, 1-inch-diameter
Round-nose pliers
Bent-nose pliers (optional)
Wire nippers

Finished Sizes
Necklace
16 inches (including clasp)
Earrings
1⅜ inches long

Instructions
Necklace
1. Use round-nose pliers to form a small loop at one end of 5-inch length of 20-gauge wire. Make sure loop is large enough to fit on necklace chain.

2. Bend wire at a 90-degree angle ⅛ inch from loop. Form long wire tail into a 1-inch circle, using 1-inch dowel rod to help maintain shape. Continue wrapping the long wire tail around in 1-inch circles. When there is a short wire tail left, wrap wire around the straight ⅛-inch portion at top of circle three times, forming a wrapped loop. This will be the support base of the wire nest.
3. Wrap the 60-inch length of 26-gauge wire into a 1-inch circle, wrapping the wire two or three times. Use dowel rod if needed to help maintain shape.
4. Place the 20-gauge 1-inch circle inside the 26-gauge 1-inch circle with the wrapped loop extending out at top. Randomly begin to wrap the remaining wire tail of the 26-gauge circle around the edges of the 20-gauge circle to secure the nest; weave wire back and forth on back to create a "floor." Continue until there are approximately 12 inches of 26-gauge wire left.
5. String a pearl on wire tail; insert wire through floor of nest and back through to front. In the same manner, string seven more pearls inside nest. Continue weaving wire in and out to fill in any holes or bare spots. To secure wire, wrap wire end tightly around another wire.
6. Slide wrapped loop onto necklace chain.

CONTINUED ON PAGE 44

Nesting Instincts
Continued from page 42

Earrings

1. Repeat steps 1 and 2 of Necklace with a 4-inch length of 20-gauge wire, forming wire into a ½-inch circle.
2. Wrap the 36-inch length of 26-gauge wire into a ½-inch circle, wrapping wire in the same manner as in step 3 of Necklace.
3. Repeat step 4 of Necklace, placing the 20-gauge ½-inch circle inside the 26-gauge ½-inch circle. In the same manner as in step 5 of Necklace, string three pearls inside wire nest. Secure wire in the same manner as before.
4. Open loop on ear wire and slide on nest.
5. Repeat steps 1–4 for a second earring.

Antiquing Jewellery (optional)
Follow these steps to oxidize jewellery which darkens the wire (as shown in photos.)

1. Peel a hard-boiled egg and cut into quarter-size pieces.
2. Place egg pieces, along with the jewellery, into a plastic container. Make sure not to let any egg pieces touch the jewellery. Put lid on container and let sit for a few hours or until desired darkness is achieved.
3. Remove jewellery from container and rinse with water. Wipe jewellery with polishing cloth. ■

SOURCE: Potato pearls, sterling silver wire, ear wires and necklace chain from Artbeads.com.

Copper Dreams
Continued from page 36

Flatten and fold the crimp tube. Trim excess wire. Repeat step 4.
8. Open a jump ring and slide on a heart charm and a crystal golden shadow charm from step 2; attach jump ring to jump ring on bracelet; close ring.
9. Open another jump ring and slide on a heart charm and a Pacific opal charm; attach this jump ring to previous jump ring, threading the jump ring between the charms on previous ring. Add two additional jump rings in the same manner, alternating between golden shadow charm and Pacific opal charm. Open remaining jump ring and slide on coil charm from step 1; attach ring to last jump ring.
10. Check back through jump rings, ensuring they are closed. ■

SOURCES: Crystal beads from Swarovski North America; copper wire and findings from Beadalon.

Effervescence
Continued from page 38

3. Open another 6mm snap-close jump ring; slide ring onto bottom of linkable ring attached to ear wire. Slide jump ring through a second linkable ring and a ruby cube head pin; close ring.
4. Open a 6mm snap-close jump ring and slide on a clear cube head pin; attach ring to bottom of second linkable ring. Close jump ring.
5. Repeat steps 2–4 for a second earring. ■

SOURCES: Snap-close jump rings, linkable rings, Venetian cubes and clasp from Via Murano; 18-gauge jump rings from Urban Maille Chainworks; bead caps and ear wires from The Bead Shop.

Filigree Butterfly
Continued from page 40

beads. Wrap and tuck wire ends under each other on back of wings a couple times to secure. Trim wire ends.

4. String a crimp bead ½ inch from one end of one 12-inch beading wire; insert short wire end through top loop of butterfly wing and back through crimp bead. Use crimp pliers to flatten and fold the crimp bead.

5. String the following, covering the crimp bead and short wire end: 5mm gold filigree round, 8mm cloisonné bead, 5mm gold filigree round and a pink oval. Repeat three additional times.

6. String a 3mm gold filigree round, 5mm cloisonné round, 3mm gold filigree round and a pink oval. Repeat twice. String a 3mm gold filigree round, 5mm cloisonné round and a 3mm gold filigree round.

7. String a crimp bead. Insert wire through one half of clasp and back through the crimp bead and a few other beads. Flatten and fold the crimp bead. Trim excess wire.

8. Repeat steps 4–7 on other side of butterfly.

Earrings
1. Slide a pink oval, 6mm cloisonné bead and a 3mm gold filigree round on a head pin; form a loop after last bead. Trim excess wire. Repeat once.
2. Open loops on head pins and attach to loops on ear wires; close loops. ■

SOURCES: Czech pressed glass beads from Blue Moon Beads; filigree beads from Hirschberg Schutz & Co. Inc.; cloisonné beads from Expo International Inc.; ear wires, clasp, filigree fans and beading wire from Cousin Corp. of America; crimp beads from Beadalon; 26-gauge wire from NSI Innovations.

Timely Reflections
Continued from page 28

cloisonné bead and a gold filigree bead.
9. String beaded eye pin from step 3. Repeat beading sequence from step 8, only in reverse. String a crimp tube. Pass wire through the left hole and referring to photo, check to make sure beaded length on front is correct. If needed,

adjust number of 2mm gold round beads to accommodate mirror size.
10. Flatten the crimp bead next to the last 2mm gold round bead. String another crimp tube and flatten it approximately 1½ inches from previous crimp tube.
11. String remaining beads in desired pattern until wire measures correct hanging length. To finish, string a crimp tube; pass wire end through top jump ring on watch face and back through crimp tube and several other beads. Crimp and flatten the crimp tube. Trim excess wire. ■

SOURCES: Swarovski crystals from Swarovski North America; watch face and cloisonné beads from Bead Time Inc.; filigree beads, head pins, jump rings and gold round beads from Fire Mountain Gems and Beads; beading wire and crimp tubes from Beadalon; mirror from Darice Inc.

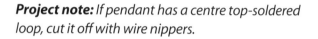

Colourful Flutters

It just isn't summer until the butterflies waft in on a warm breeze. Wear one of the heralds of summer around your neck until the warm days arrive.

DESIGNS BY CANDIE COOPER

Skill Level: Easy

Materials
Cloisonné butterfly pendant with antennae loops
5 (12mm) blue butterfly beads
10 (6mm) padparadscha Swarovski crystal round beads
6 (6mm) blue glass round beads
29 (3mm) gold round beads
22 (5mm) peach flower spacer beads
20 (4mm) peridot Swarovski crystal bicone beads
8 (8mm) green floral cloisonné beads
4 (1.3mm) gold crimp beads
4 (4mm) gold crimp covers
3 (2-inch) gold ball-and-star–tipped head pins
2 gold ear wires
Gold lobster-claw clasp
2 inches gold linked chain
2 (9-inch) lengths 19-strand .018-inch-diameter gold nylon-coated flexible beading wire
Round-nose pliers
Flat-nose pliers
Crimp pliers
Wire nippers

Finished Sizes
Necklace
16⅜ inches (including clasp)
Earrings
1¼ inches long

Project note: *If pendant has a centre top-soldered loop, cut it off with wire nippers.*

Instructions
Necklace
1. Slide a butterfly bead and a gold round bead onto a head pin; use round-nose pliers to form a loop above top bead. Trim excess wire. Open loop and attach to end of gold chain; close loop. Set aside.
2. String a crimp bead onto one 9-inch wire ½ inch from one end; place wire end through one loop on butterfly's antennae and back through the crimp bead. Use crimp pliers to flatten and fold the crimp bead. Attach a crimp cover over crimp bead.
3. String a peach flower, padparadscha bead, peach flower, gold round bead, green cloisonné bead, gold round bead, peridot bead, blue butterfly bead, peridot bead and a gold round bead. Repeat once.
4. String a peach flower, padparadscha bead, peach flower, gold round bead, green cloisonné bead and a gold round bead.
5. String a peridot bead, blue glass round bead, peridot bead, gold round bead, peach flower, padparadscha bead, peach flower and a gold round bead. Repeat once.
6. String a peridot bead, blue glass round bead, peridot bead and a gold round bead.
7. String a crimp bead; place wire end through end link on chain from step 1 and back through crimp

CONTINUED ON PAGE 80

Peachy Blush

Wrap yourself in the luxury of luscious pink coral. Why not? This spectacular set is easy to make!

DESIGNS BY DIANNE DE VIENNE

Skill Level: Easy

Materials
98 (12–20mm) coral teardrop beads
16-inch strand small branch coral
4 (5mm) sterling silver tube beads
2 sterling silver soldered jump rings
4 sterling silver crimp beads
2 sterling silver ear wires
2 (12mm) sterling silver lobster-claw clasps
12 inches 24-gauge sterling silver round wire
38 inches .018-inch-diameter nylon-coated
    flexible beading wire
Round-nose pliers
Chain-nose pliers
Crimp pliers
Wire nippers

Finished Sizes
Necklace
17¼ inches (including clasp)
Bracelet
7¼ inches (including clasp)
Earrings
2⅛ inches long

Instructions
Necklace
1. Cut a 24-inch length of beading wire. String a crimp bead ½ inch from one end; place short wire tail through lobster-claw clasp and back through crimp bead. Use crimp pliers to flatten the crimp bead.
2. String a tube bead. String a branch coral bead and a coral teardrop; repeat 68 additional times. String a branch coral bead and a tube bead.
3. String a crimp bead; place wire end through a jump ring and back through crimp bead and tube bead. Flatten the crimp bead; trim excess wire.

Bracelet
1. Repeat step 1 of Necklace with a 14-inch length of beading wire.
2. String a tube bead. String a branch coral bead and a coral teardrop; repeat 22 additional times. String a branch coral bead and a tube bead.
3. Repeat step 3 of Necklace.

Earrings

1. Cut sterling silver wire into two 1½-inch lengths, two 2-inch lengths and two 2½-inch lengths.

2. Insert one 1½-inch wire through a coral teardrop, positioning teardrop ½ inch from one end. Bring both wire ends above teardrop and wrap short wire tail around wire, forming a wrapped loop. String a branch coral bead onto wire; form a wrapped loop above bead. Trim excess wire. Repeat once.

3. Repeat step 2 with 2-inch wires, only string ⅜ inch of branch coral beads instead of a single branch coral bead. Repeat step 2 with 2½-inch wire, only string ¾ inch of branch coral beads instead of a single branch coral bead.

4. Open loops on ear wires and slide three wires, one of each length, onto each loop. Close loops. ■

SOURCES: Coral beads from AAA Earth Treasures; sterling silver wire from Fire Mountain Gems and Beads.

Passion's Poem

Well-known lampwork artist Lisa Kan creates her famous "Haiku" beads in many beautiful colours. The colour red is not only poetic, it also symbolizes passion.

DESIGN BY JEAN YATES

Skill Level: Easy

Materials
Dark red Haiku glass bead
60 (6mm) black cubic zirconia coin beads
16-inch strand 4mm labradorite faceted round beads
16-inch strand sterling silver Bali hex spacers
8mm kambaba rondelle
Swarovski crystal beads: 2 (6mm) jet round, 1 (8mm) morion cube
Pewter dragonfly link
2 (6mm) sterling silver twisted closed jump rings
3-inch 20-gauge sterling silver head pin
4 (3mm) sterling silver crimp beads
Sterling silver or pewter toggle clasp
6 inches 18-gauge sterling silver dead-soft wire
2 (28-inch) lengths .014-inch-diameter nylon-coated flexible beading wire
Round-nose pliers
Chain-nose pliers
Wire nippers

Finished Size
17¼ inches (including clasp), plus a 4½-inch droplet

Instructions
1. Form a ³⁄₁₆-inch wrapped loop at one end of 6-inch sterling silver wire, attaching loop to top loop of dragonfly link before wrapping.
2. String the Haiku bead, twisted jump ring and a jet crystal.

3. Form another ³⁄₁₆-inch wrapped loop above crystal. Trim excess wire.
4. Slide the following on a head pin: sterling silver hex spacer, jet crystal, morion cube, twisted jump ring, kambaba rondelle and a sterling silver hex spacer. Form a wrapped loop above last bead, attaching loop to bottom loop of dragonfly link before wrapping. Trim excess wire. This completes the pendant; set aside.
5. String a crimp bead ½ inch from one end of one 28-inch beading wire; place short wire end through one half of clasp and back through crimp bead. Use chain-nose pliers to flatten the crimp bead.
6. String 30 black coin beads, pendant and 30 black coin beads.
7. String a crimp bead. Place wire through remaining half of clasp and back through crimp bead. Flatten the crimp bead. Trim excess wire.
8. Repeat step 5 to attach second 28-inch wire to one half of clasp.
9. String six labradorite round beads and 10 sterling silver hex spacers; repeat three additional times. String three labradorite round beads.
10. Insert wire through top loop of pendant. Repeat step 9 in reverse to string remaining half of strand.
11. Repeat step 7. ■

SOURCES: Haiku bead from Lisa Kan Designs; cubic zirconia coin beads and Swarovski crystal beads from Fusion Beads; kambaba rondelle from GemMall.com; labradorite and Bali hex spacer strands from The Bead Shop; dragonfly link from Green Girl Studios; twisted jump rings from Jewelry Supply Inc.; toggle clasp and Twisted Tornado Crimp® beads from Via Murano.

Wish ...

Close your eyes and make a wish! A colourful celebration of wonder and whimsy, this necklace will transport you back to the carefree summer days of youth.

DESIGN BY MARGOT POTTER

Skill Level: Intermediate

Materials

1¼-inch-square clear tile
Dandelion rubber stamp
Black archival ink pad
Black fine-tip permanent marker
23 (½-inch-long) faceted carnelian tube beads
6 (10mm) lime green Lucite or cat's-eye glass round beads
24 (6mm) rose alabaster Swarovski crystal bicone beads
6 (12mm) dyed orange quartz lentil beads
22 (3mm) silver-plated spacers
Silver-plated jump rings: 1 (10mm), 14 (4mm)
12 silver-plated eye pins
2 silver-plated scrimp findings
3 lime green porcelain round links
3-strand lime green porcelain clasp
12 inches silver-plated small rolo chain
20 inches .015-inch-diameter nylon-coated flexible beading wire
Mini screwdriver
Round-nose pliers
2 pairs needle-nose pliers (optional)
Flush cutters

Finished Size

14½ inches (including clasp), with a 2-inch extender

Instructions

Bottom Strand

1. Stamp dandelion on tile, being careful to not slide the stamp across tile surface. Allow tile to dry. Use fine-tip marker to write "wish…" along bottom edge of tile; let dry.

2. Open 10mm jump ring and slide on stamped tile; attach ring to a lime green porcelain link. Close ring. **Note:** *If needed, use both needle-nose pliers to help open and close jump rings.* Use 4mm jump rings to attach remaining lime green porcelain links to top loop on first porcelain link. This will be the centre of the bottom beaded strand.

3. Slide the following on an eye pin: rose alabaster bicone bead, lime green round bead and a rose alabaster bicone bead. Use round-nose pliers to form a loop after last bead; trim excess wire. Repeat five additional times for a total of six lime green/rose links.

4. Repeat step 3 with the following beads to make a total of six orange/rose links: rose alabaster bicone bead, orange quartz lentil bead and a rose alabaster bicone bead.

5. Open a 4mm jump ring and slide on a lime green/rose link; attach ring to one of the top lime green porcelain links; close ring. Open another 4mm jump ring and attach to opposite loop on the lime green/rose link; slide on an orange/rose link. Close ring. In the same manner, continue attaching

CONTINUED ON PAGE 80

Deep Blue Sea

Midnight blue blister pearls and shell charms evoke the mystery of the ocean in a striking necklace that will give any outfit understated nautical appeal.

DESIGN BY DIANNE DE VIENNE

Skill Level: Beginner

Materials

40 blue blister pearl briolettes
9 silver shell charms
20 (4mm) sterling silver round beads
2 (6mm) sterling silver tube beads
9 (4–5mm) silver jump rings
2 (1.3mm) silver crimp beads
Sterling silver toggle clasp
23 inches .018-inch-diameter nylon-coated flexible beading wire
Chain-nose pliers
Wire nippers

Finished Size

16½ inches (including clasp)

Instructions

1. Attach a jump ring to each shell charm.
2. String a crimp bead ½ inch from one end of beading wire; place wire end through one half of clasp and back through crimp bead. Use crimp pliers to flatten and fold the crimp bead.
3. String a silver tube bead and a silver round bead.
4. String four blue blister pearls, silver round bead, shell charm and a silver round bead. Repeat eight additional times. String four blue blister pearls, silver round bead and a silver tube bead.
5. String a crimp bead; thread wire through other half of clasp and back through crimp bead, and tube and round beads. Flatten and fold the crimp bead. Trim excess wire. ■

SOURCES: Blister pearl briolettes from Pizazz Works; shell charms and sterling silver beads from South Pacific Wholesale Co.

Nautical Pearls

This navy blue, gold and clear crystal necklace has the look of knotted cord, but uses seed beads for easy stringing.

DESIGN BY MOLLY SCHALLER

Skill Level: Easy

Materials
Navy blue Swarovski crystal pearls: 2 (8mm), 23 (12mm)
30mm clear Swarovski crystal cosmic ring
27 (15/0) metallic navy blue seed beads
2 (1.3mm) gold crimp tubes
2 gold Wire Guardians
2 (3.5mm) gold oval Scrimp findings
2-ring gold lobster-claw clasp
2 (¾-inch) lengths medium .028-inch-diameter .925 gold-plated French wire
22 inches .018-inch-diameter 19-strand satin gold nylon-coated flexible beading wire
Scrimp Tool Kit
Crimp tool
Flush cutters

Finished Size
15½ inches (including clasp)

Instructions
1. Cut one 10-inch length and one 12-inch length of beading wire.
2. Onto the shorter wire, string a Scrimp finding, Wire Guardian and one half of clasp 1 inch from end.
3. Pass short wire tail back through the Scrimp finding and use Scrimp tool to secure the wire within the Scrimp. Trim short wire tail.
4. String one seed bead, 8mm pearl and a seed bead. String eight 12mm pearls, stringing a seed bead after each.
5. String a crimp tube and one ¾-inch length of French wire.
6. Pass the wire through the centre of the cosmic ring and back through the crimp tube. Pull wire gently to secure the French wire around the ring. Use crimp pliers to flatten and fold the crimp tube. Trim excess wire.
7. Repeat steps 2–6 with 12-inch wire, stringing all the remaining pearls in the same pattern as before. ∎

SOURCES: Crystal pearls and cosmic ring from Swarovski North America; seed beads from Fire Mountain Gems and Beads; beading wire, French wire and findings from Beadalon.

Rainbow Braids

Make this fun necklace using bright colours that will give your wardrobe a citrus punch.

DESIGN BY CAROLE RODGERS

Skill Level: Easy

Materials

11/0 seed beads: pink silver-lined, green matte, light turquoise, black, yellow pearlescent, orange matte, 4–5 grams each colour

8/0 seed beads: pink lustre, green silver-lined, turquoise, orange AB, 5–6 grams each colour

6/0 seed beads: white, yellow matte, 6–7 grams each colour

6 extra beads of any shape or size

2 (10mm) gold bell caps

3 (5mm) gold split rings

2 (2-inch) gold eye pins

Gold toggle clasp

10 yards .006-inch-diameter white beading thread

Size 12 beading needle

Round-nose pliers

Chain-nose pliers

Split-ring pliers

Side cutters

Gem glue

Finished Size

26¼ inches (including clasp)

Instructions

1. Thread needle with a 60-inch length of thread, bringing ends together; knot ends onto loop end of an eye pin, leaving a 2-inch thread tail. Apply a dot of glue to knot; let dry.

2. Begin stringing pink silver-lined 11/0 seed beads, alternating them with pink lustre 8/0 seed beads until length measures 26 inches.

3. Loosely tie an extra bead on end of thread to secure seed beads. Set aside.

4. Repeat step 1 for next strand, attaching thread to the same eye pin. Begin stringing three yellow pearlescent 11/0 seed beads, alternating them with yellow matte 6/0 seed beads until length measures 26 inches. Repeat step 3.

5. Repeat step 1 for next strand, attaching thread to the same eye pin. Begin stringing light turquoise 11/0 seed beads, alternating them with turquoise 8/0 seed beads until length measures 26 inches. Repeat step 3.

6. Repeat step 1 for next strand, attaching thread to the same eye pin. Begin stringing two green matte 11/0 seed beads, alternating them with green silver-lined 8/0 seed beads until length measures 26 inches. Repeat step 3.

7. Repeat step 1 for next strand, attaching thread to the same eye pin. Begin stringing orange matte 11/0 seed beads, alternating them with two orange AB 8/0 seed beads until length measures 26 inches. Repeat step 3.

8. Repeat step 1 for next strand, attaching thread to the same eye pin. Begin stringing black 11/0 seed beads, alternating them with white 6/0 seed beads until length measures 26 inches. Repeat step 3.

9. Separate beaded strands into three pairs; loosely braid strands together, checking for length and adding or subtracting beads if needed. **Note:** *To add or remove beads, simply remove extra bead at end of strand and string or take off beads.*

10. Remove extra bead from one strand;

CONTINUED ON PAGE 81

Plain-Jane Butterfly

Subtle and low-key, this is a perfect casual-Friday necklace. Scrimp beads anchor the lightweight pendant at the centre and keep the lobster-claw clasp in the back. Finish with a simple seed-bead loop.

DESIGN BY BARB SWITZER

Skill Level: Beginner

Materials
Small wooden butterfly pendant
6 (3mm) grey glass pearls
2 grams 11/0 grey seed beads
1½-inch silver head pin
2 Scrimp findings
2 (1.3mm) silver crimp beads
Silver lobster-claw clasp
20 inches .018-inch-diameter nylon-coated
    flexible beading wire
Round-nose pliers
Chain-nose pliers
Crimp pliers
Wire nippers
Mini screwdriver

Finished Size
16⅜ inches (including clasp)

Instructions
1. Slide a seed bead and butterfly pendant on a head pin; form a wrapped loop above butterfly. Trim excess wire. String head pin on beading wire, centring it.
2. String a pearl, nine seed beads and a pearl on each side of head pin.

3. Insert wire through a Scrimp finding; tighten Scrimp with mini screwdriver. Repeat on opposite side of necklace, making sure beads and pendant are snug and centred on wire.
4. String a pearl and 30 seed beads on each side of necklace.
5. On one end of wire, string a crimp bead, two seed beads, clasp and two seed beads. Thread wire end back through the crimp bead, pulling wire taut. On the opposite end, string a crimp bead and 16 seed beads; insert wire end back through the crimp bead to form a beaded loop large enough for clasp.
6. If needed, adjust necklace so pendant is still centred; use crimp pliers to flatten and fold the crimp beads. Trim excess wire. ■

SOURCES: Wooden butterfly from The Bead Shack; seed beads and clasp from Fusion Beads; beading wire and Scrimp findings from Beadalon.

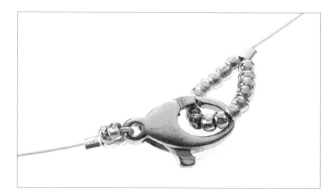

The Clustered Y

The classic Y necklace takes on a completely new dimension: unlimited, personal and convertible! Each element of the cluster is removable and interchangeable to reflect the personality of the wearer.

DESIGN BY BARBARA LYNCH

Skill Level: Easy

Materials

Assorted elements such as semi-precious stones, various beads, charms, earrings, old pendants, etc.
7 (3–4-inch) sterling silver head pins
7 sterling silver jump rings
7 small sterling silver spring-ring or lobster-claw clasps
Large sterling silver spring-ring or lobster-claw clasp
21–25 inches sterling silver chain (chain should be strong enough to support weight of assorted elements)
Round-nose pliers
Chain-nose pliers
Wire nippers

Finished Size

18–21 inches (including clasp), plus a 3–4-inch droplet

Instructions

1. String beads and/or charms on head pins as desired. Form wrapped loops after beads; trim excess wire.

2. Use a jump ring to attach beaded head pins, pendants, charms, etc., to a small spring-ring or lobster-claw clasp.

3. Attach one element to last link of chain. Attach large clasp to opposite end of chain.

4. Attach remaining elements to the last 3 to 4 inches of chain using small clasps.

5. To wear necklace, connect unadorned end of chain to a link one or two links above last link with an embellishment. ***Note:*** *Since elements are attached to necklace with small clasps, they can easily be removed and others added.* ■

Presto Change-o!

It can be intimidating to alter a design; maybe you don't know where to start. Find a design you love and decide which element to keep and which to change—size, colour, texture, materials, theme. These earrings are all built on a theme: ear wire, bead, chain, bead. After you've finished a few of these, experiment on your own!

DESIGNS BY MICHELLE MACH

Go Wild

Skill Level: Easy

Materials
2 (25mm) green shell square hoops
4 (15mm) paua shell flower beads
4 (13mm) sterling silver flower drops
Silver jump rings: 2 (6mm), 2 (4 x 3mm) oval
2 blue niobium ear wires
Silver chain: 2 (1-inch) lengths cable, 2 (2-inch)
   lengths oval-linked
Chain-nose pliers
Wire nippers

Finished Size
3 inches long

Instructions
1. Open loop on an ear wire and slide on one end of 1-inch cable chain; wrap chain around one corner of green hoop. Slide other end of chain onto open ear wire; close loop.
2. Open an oval jump ring and attach one end of 2-inch oval-linked chain; wrap chain around opposite corner of green hoop. Slide opposite end of chain onto jump ring. Attach a paua shell flower and a silver flower drop on jump ring. Close ring.

3. Use wire nippers to cut off loop on another silver flower drop. Open a 6mm jump ring and slide on a paua shell flower and the silver flower drop with no loop. Attach jump ring to front and back centre links of oval-linked chain. Close jump ring.

4. Repeat steps 1–3 for second earring.

Flower Power

Skill Level: Easy

Materials

2 (25 x 3mm) glass multicoloured millefiori go-go beads

2 (28mm) white shell carved flower pendants

2 (4 x 3mm) silver oval jump rings

2 (14 x 20mm) sterling silver oval hoop earrings

2 (2-inch) lengths silver flat figure-8 chain

Chain-nose pliers

Wire nippers

Finished Size

3 inches long

Instructions

1. Open hoop earring and slide on a go-go bead; close hoop.

2. Open a jump ring and attach it to a shell flower pendant and one end of a 2-inch chain. Wrap chain around bottom of go-go bead and slide other chain end onto jump ring. Close jump ring.

3. Repeat steps 1 and 2 for second earring.

Silver Swirl

Skill Level: Easy

Materials

2 (22mm) silver patterned square discs

2 (25mm) silver swirl toggle clasps (swirl round ends only)

2 (4mm) silver jump rings

2 (14 x 20mm) sterling silver oval hoop earrings

2 (1-inch) lengths silver oval-linked chain

Chain-nose pliers

Wire nippers

Finished Size

2¾ inches long

Instructions

1. Open a hoop earring and slide on a swirl drop; close hoop.

2. Open a jump ring and attach silver disc; slide one end of a 1-inch chain onto ring. Wrap chain around bottom of swirl drop and slide other chain end onto jump ring. Close ring.

3. Repeat steps 1 and 2 for second earring. ■

SOURCES: Paua shells, silver flower drops, go-go beads, shell flower pendants, jump rings, oval hoops, sterling silver oval hoop earrings and chain from Fire Mountain Gems and Beads; green square hoops from Bead Happy; blue niobium ear wires and silver square discs from Loveland Bead Co.; swirl toggle clasps from Thunderbird Supply Co.

Hip Hoops

Your inner flower child will love Stephanie Sersich's flower beads.

DESIGN BY KATIE HACKER

Skill Level: Easy

Materials

2 (20mm) orange lampwork flower beads
4 (4mm) peridot Swarovski crystal round beads
6mm Swarovski crystal bicone beads: 2 peridot, 2 light sapphire
4 clear bead bumpers
2 (6mm) silver jump rings
4 silver ball-and-star–tipped head pins
2 (1-inch) silver beading hoops
5½ inches silver small cable chain
Round-nose pliers
Chain-nose pliers
Wire nippers

Finished Size

3 inches long

Instructions

1. Cut two 1¼-inch lengths and two 1½-inch lengths of chain.

2. Open a jump ring and slide on end links of one 1¼-inch chain and one 1½-inch chain; close jump ring. Repeat once.

3. Slide a light sapphire bicone bead onto a head pin; use round-nose pliers to form a wrapped head-pin loop above bead, attaching loop to end link of one 1¼-inch chain before wrapping. Trim excess wire. Repeat once.

4. Slide a peridot bicone bead onto a head pin; form a wrapped head-pin loop above bead, attaching loop to end link of a 1½-inch chain before wrapping. Trim excess wire. Repeat once.

5. Slide the following onto a beading hoop: bead bumper, peridot round bead, jump ring with attached chains, flower bead, peridot round bead and a bead bumper. ***Note:** The flower bead should be strung with back of flower facing jump ring.*

6. Use chain-nose pliers to carefully bend the end of beading hoop into a right angle so hoop can be closed.

7. Repeat steps 5 and 6 for second earring. ■

SOURCES: Flower beads from Stephanie Sersich; beading hoops, bead bumpers, chain and head pins from Beadalon; Swarovski crystals from Absolute Crystal Components Inc.

Pink Pizzazz

You'll be all dressed up ready for a fun night on the town with these flirty loops.

DESIGN BY CAROLE RODGERS

Skill Level: Easy

Materials
2 loops silver bracelet memory wire
68 (2.5mm) silver round beads
48 (4mm) silver Bali daisy spacers
50 (11 x 6mm) pink flat top-drilled oval beads
2 (5mm) silver split rings
2 silver ear wires
Round-nose pliers
Chain-nose pliers
Split-ring pliers
Heavy-duty wire cutters or memory wire shears

Finished Size
3¼ inches long

Project note: *Memory wire is hard to cut and will damage regular wire nippers. Always use memory wire shears to cut wire coils.*

Instructions
1. Cut memory wire in half, forming two hoops. Use round-nose pliers to form a small loop at one end of each hoop. Loops should face in toward centre of hoops.
2. String 17 silver round beads. String a flat oval bead and a daisy spacer; repeat 23 additional times. String a flat oval bead and 17 silver round beads. Form a small loop facing in toward centre of hoop after last bead.
3. Repeat step 2 for other hoop.
4. Attach both loops of one hoop to a split ring; attach split ring to ear wire. Repeat for second hoop. ∎

SOURCES: Memory wire, split rings and ear wires from Beadalon; flat oval beads from Wild Things Beads.

Crystal Acrobatics

Sun-kissed sparkles cascade through silver rings in these dazzling dangle earrings.

DESIGN BY CAITO AMOROSE

Skill Level: Intermediate

Materials
Swarovski crystal bicone beads: 2 (8mm) jonquil, 4 (6mm) sun, 4 (6mm) topaz, 16 (4mm) jonquil, 4 (4mm) topaz, 4 (4mm) sun
Sterling silver 4-hole open rings: 2 (17.5mm), 2 (13.5mm)
2 (4mm) sterling silver split rings
10 sterling silver eye pins
8 sterling silver head pins
2 sterling silver ear wires
20 inches 24-gauge sterling silver wire
12 inches 1.6mm sterling silver cable chain
Round-nose pliers
Chain-nose pliers
Wire nippers

Finished Size
4¼ inches long

Instructions
1. Cut chain as follows: eight ¾-inch lengths, eight ½-inch lengths and eight ¼-inch lengths. Cut sixteen 1¼-inch pieces of wire.
2. Use round-nose pliers to form a wrapped loop ½ inch from one end of a 1¼-inch wire, attaching a ¾-inch wire inside loop before wrapping. String a 4mm jonquil crystal on wire; insert wire through one hole in a 17.5mm ring. Form another wrapped loop, attaching a ½-inch chain before wrapping. Trim excess wire.

3. Repeat step 2 to attach a 4mm topaz crystal to 13.5mm ring. Add ¼-inch chain before finishing last wrapped loop.
4. Slide a 6mm topaz crystal on an eye pin; form a wrapped loop, attaching loop to end link of previous ¼-inch chain before wrapping. Trim excess wire. Slide a 4mm jonquil crystal on a head pin; form a wrapped loop above crystal. Trim excess wire. Open loop on bottom of eye pin; attach jonquil head pin; close loop.
5. Repeat steps 2–4, substituting a 4mm sun crystal in place of jonquil crystal (step 2); substitute a 4mm jonquil crystal in place of topaz crystal (step 3); substitute a 4mm jonquil in place of 6mm topaz crystal and a 6mm sun crystal in place of 4mm jonquil crystal (step 4).
6. Repeat steps 2–4. Repeat step 5.
7. Attach four loose ends of ¾-inch chains to split ring; attach split ring to loop on an eye pin. Slide an 8mm jonquil crystal and a 4mm sun crystal on eye pin. Form a loop above top crystal; trim excess wire. Open loop and attach to ear wire; close loop.
8. Repeat steps 2–7 for second earring. ■

SOURCE: All materials from Fire Mountain Gems and Beads.

Lots of Knots

Creating ball-knot beads is a breeze with Clover's template.

DESIGNS BY CANDIE COOPER

Skill Level: Easy

Materials
Porcelain cat beads: 4 (9 x 9mm), 3 (13 x 13mm)
Round beads: 16 (4mm) coral, 15 (3.2mm) silver, 10 (6mm) pink
7 (5mm) silver bead caps
2 (1.3mm) silver crimp beads
2 (3mm) silver crimp covers (optional)
7 (2-inch) silver head pins
2 silver ear wires
12mm silver toggle clasp
Ball Knot template
3 yards medium blue thin cord
12 inches .018-inch-diameter 49-strand nylon-coated flexible beading wire
Tapestry needle
Round-nose pliers
Flat-nose pliers
Crimp pliers
Wire nippers
Fabric glue

Finished Sizes
Bracelet
8 inches (including clasp)
Earrings
1⅜ inches long

Instructions
Bracelet
1. Following manufacturer's instructions, use Ball Knot template to create eight ball knots with blue cord. Seal knot ends with fabric glue; let dry.

2. Slide a bead cap, a small cat bead and a silver round bead on a head pin; use round-nose pliers to form a loop above top bead. Trim excess wire. Repeat for all three large cat beads and one more small cat bead for a total of five beaded head pins.
3. String a crimp bead ½ inch from one end of beading wire; place wire end through one half of clasp and back through crimp bead. Use crimp pliers to flatten and fold the crimp bead.
4. String a coral round bead. Insert wire through tapestry needle and string a ball knot; remove needle once knot is on wire.
5. String a pink round bead, silver round bead, coral round bead, small cat head pin, coral round bead, silver round bead and a pink round bead. In the same manner as in step 4, string a ball knot.
6. Repeat step 5 three times, substituting the large cat head pins in place of small cat head pins. Repeat step 5. String a coral round bead.
7. String a crimp bead; place wire end through remaining half of clasp and back through crimp bead. Flatten and fold the crimp bead. Trim excess wire. If desired, attach crimp covers over crimp beads.

CONTINUED ON PAGE 81

A-Luring Bracelet

When you visit the sporting-goods store, be sure to look for items to use as jewellery components. This bracelet uses spinner blades that are used on fishing lures!

DESIGN BY CAROLE RODGERS

Skill Level: Easy

Materials
⅞-inch Premium Indiana fishing spinner blades,
  10 of each colour: silver diamond, gold
  diamond, copper diamond
Silver jump rings: 22 (10mm), 93 (4mm)
Medium silver lobster-claw clasp
2 pairs chain-nose pliers

Finished Size
9⅛ inches (including clasp) Bracelet can be
  adjusted to fit most wrists.

Instructions
1. Make sure all 10mm jump rings are closed and smooth to the touch. Use both pairs of pliers to open a 4mm jump ring; attach two 10mm jump rings with open 4mm jump ring. Close ring. Repeat two additional times, connecting the two additional 4mm jump rings to the same 10mm jump rings. The two 10mm jump rings should now be connected with three 4mm jump rings. Continue to connect 10mm jump rings together in this same manner until all 10mm jump rings have been used, creating a bracelet chain. **Note:** *If a shorter length is desired, do not connect all 10mm jump rings. Sample bracelet used all 10mm jump rings to provide extra rings on one side as an extender.*

2. Open 10mm jump ring at end of chain and slide on lobster-claw clasp; close ring.

3. Set aside one spinner blade of each colour. Open a 4mm jump ring and slide on a silver spinner blade; attach ring to second link from clasp. Close ring. In the same manner, attach a copper spinner blade to next link. Continue attaching silver and copper spinner blades to chain, alternating between the two.

4. Use 4mm jump rings to attach gold spinner blades to the 4mm jump rings that connect the 10mm jump rings.

5. Attach remaining three spinner blades to end link. ∎

SOURCES: Spinner blades from Cabela's Inc.; jump rings and clasp from Beadalon.

Ocean Dreams

Czech glass in opaque, clear and two-tone shades, replicates the colours of ocean waves.

DESIGN BY LISETTA COFFIN

Skill Level: Beginner

Materials

Czech glass faceted rondelle beads: 6 (4 x 7mm) turquoise/bronze, 4 (4 x 7mm) green peridot opal, 2 (6 x 9mm) blue aqua, 4 (6 x 9mm) green peridot opal, 2 (6 x 9mm) two-tone opaque green peridot

8 (4mm) gold faceted bicone spacer beads

14 gold seed beads

4 (1.3mm) gold crimp beads

Gold watch face

Gold toggle clasp

2 (9-inch) lengths .014-inch-diameter 49-strand nylon-coated flexible beading wire

Crimp pliers

Wire nippers

Finished Size

8 inches (including clasp)

Instructions

1. String one 9-inch length of beading wire through loop on one side of watch face, leaving a 2-inch wire tail on one side.

2. String a gold seed bead on each side of wire; with wires together, string a gold seed bead, forming a triangle with all three seed beads (Fig. 1). With wires together, string a crimp bead; use crimp pliers to flatten the crimp bead.

3. Onto the long wire, string the following, running both wires through the first couple of beads: turquoise/bronze rondelle, gold bicone spacer, 6 x 9mm green peridot opal rondelle, blue aqua rondelle and a 6 x 9mm green peridot opal rondelle. String a gold bicone spacer, turquoise/bronze rondelle, 4 x 7mm green peridot opal rondelle, gold bicone spacer, two-tone green peridot rondelle, gold bicone spacer, 4 x 7mm green peridot opal rondelle and a turquoise/bronze rondelle.

4. String three gold seed beads, crimp bead and a gold seed bead; place wire end through one half of clasp and back through seed beads, crimp bead and several other beads. Flatten the crimp bead. Trim excess wire.

5. Repeat steps 1–4 for other side of watch. ■

SOURCES: Czech rondelle beads from Beadbabe.com; gold spacer beads from Rings & Things; Accu-Flex beading wire and clasp from Fire Mountain Gems and Beads.

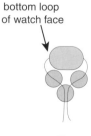

bottom loop of watch face

Fig. 1

Summer Jewels

Hot, hot, hot jewel tones complement any outfit!
This multifunctional eyeglasses strap easily
converts to a necklace or bracelet to fit any
occasion—and it's perfect for a woman on the go.

DESIGN BY CAITO AMOROSE

Skill Level: Intermediate

Materials
44 (6mm) gold-plated Swarovski crystal links in
   various colours
86 (8/0) glass seed beads in various colours
Gold jump rings: 43 (6mm), 2 (4mm)
2 gold eyeglasses holders
2 (6mm) gold lobster-claw clasps (clasp sides only)
Jump-ring tool or chain-nose pliers

Finished Size
30 inches

Project note: *To convert eyeglasses strap into a
necklace or bracelet, simply remove the eyeglasses
holders and attach lobster-claw clasps to each other.
Makes one single-strand necklace or double for a
shorter length; wrap around wrist four times to wear
as a bracelet.*

Instructions
1. Open a 4mm jump ring; slide on a lobster-claw
clasp and a crystal link. Close ring.
2. Open a 6mm jump ring; slide on a seed bead,
opposite end of previous crystal link, seed bead
and a crystal link. Close ring.
3. Repeat step 2 until all seed beads and crystal
links have been connected.

4. Open a 4mm jump ring;
slide on remaining lobster-
claw clasp. Attach jump ring to last
crystal link; close ring.
5. Open each clasp to attach an
eyeglasses holder to each
end. ■

SOURCE: All materials from Fire
Mountain Gems and Beads.

Catch of the Day Frame

Frame your summer memories with cerulean and sea green glass beads.

DESIGN BY MARY AYRES

Skill Level: Easy

Materials
Unfinished wooden frame with a wide front
Fishnet
Light blue printed paper
Blue bead mix
Blue seed beads
1½-inch silver head pins
Brown thread
Fine sandpaper
Blue dye ink pad
Blue acrylic paint
Craft sponge or paper towel
Paintbrush
Sewing needle
Round-nose pliers
Fabric glue

Instructions

1. Place frame face down on reverse side of a sheet of light blue printed paper; trace around inner and outer edges. Cut out paper frame; use craft sponge or paper towel to ink edges.

2. Cut a piece of fishnet slightly larger than frame front; glue fishnet to paper frame, applying glue to outside edges only. Trim fishnet around frame opening and outside edges as needed.

3. Referring to photo, hand-sew seed beads to fishnet around inner and outer edges. To do this, first use sewing needle to poke holes on both sides of fishnet where seed bead will be attached; beginning from the back, insert thread through one hole and string a seed bead. **Note:** *If seed bead will not fit over eye of needle, remove needle from thread and then string seed bead.* Insert thread through other hole to back. Knot thread ends on back. Repeat for each seed bead.

4. Paint inner and outer edges and back of wooden frame blue; let dry. Lightly sand frame for a distressed appearance.

5. Adhere paper frame to front of wooden frame. Let dry. Glue inner edges of fishnet to frame.

6. Slide a bead on a head pin; bend top of head pin over slightly and attach head pin to fishnet as shown; continue bending top of head pin until top meets top of bead, securing head pin to fishnet. Repeat as desired. ■

SOURCES: Printed paper from BasicGrey; beads from Blue Moon Beads; fabric glue from Beacon Adhesives Inc.

Colourful Flutters
Continued from page 46

bead and several other beads. Flatten and fold the crimp bead. Trim excess wire. Attach a crimp cover over crimp bead.

8. Repeat steps 2–6 to string other half of necklace. Repeat step 7, attach wire end to clasp instead of chain.

Earrings

1. Slide a green cloisonné bead, peach flower and a gold round bead onto a head pin; form a loop above bead. Repeat once.

2. Open loops and attach to ear wires. ■

SOURCE: Cloisonné pendant and cloisonné beads from Fire Mountain Gems and Beads; beading wire and head pins from Beadalon.

Wish ...
Continued from page 52

the following links to make one side of necklace: lime green/rose link, orange/rose link, lime green/ rose link and an orange/rose link. Repeat for other side of necklace.

6. Open loop on last link and attach to bottom link on one half of 3-strand clasp; close loop. Repeat

to attach opposite end loop to bottom link on remaining half of clasp.

Centre Strand

1. Slide one end of wire through scrimp finding; insert wire through centre link on one half of clasp and back through scrimp finding. Use mini screwdriver to secure scrimp to wire.

2. Beginning with a carnelian tube bead, string all carnelian tubes and all silver spacers, alternating between the two. Strand should begin and end with a carnelian tube.

3. Attach wire to centre link on remaining half of clasp in the same manner as in step 1.

Finishing

1. Open end links on rolo chain, attach to top links on both halves of clasp; close links.

2. Check back through necklace to ensure all jump rings are securely closed. ■

SOURCES: Clear tile from Junkitz; rubber stamp from Inkadinkado; porcelain links and clasp from Earthenwood Studio; carnelian beads and orange quartz beads from Great Craft Works; rose alabaster beads from Swarovski North America; Lucite beads from The Beadin' Path; rolo chain, eye pins, spacers, scrimp findings and mini screwdriver from Beadalon; jump rings from Rings & Things.

Rainbow Braids
Continued from page 58

knot thread on loop of remaining eye pin. Apply a dot of glue to knot; let dry. Repeat for each strand, knotting each on the same eye pin. Trim thread ends.

11. Thread one eye pin through bell cap; use round-nose pliers to form a wrapped loop with eye pin extending from bell cap. Trim excess wire. Repeat for opposite end of necklace.

12. Use split ring to attach one end of necklace to round half of clasp. Use two split rings to attach bar end of clasp to opposite end of necklace. ■

SOURCES: Beading thread from Beadalon; gem glue from Beacon Adhesives Inc.

Lot of Knots
Continued from page 70

Earrings

1. Slide a bead cap, small cat bead, coral round bead, ball knot and a coral round bead on a head pin; form a loop above top bead. Trim excess wire. Repeat once.

2. Open loops on ear wires and attach beaded head pins; close loops. ■

SOURCES: Ball Knot template, blue cord and fabric glue from Clover Needlecraft Inc.; beading wire, clasp, crimp beads and crimp covers from Beadalon.

Stag's Bride

Fit for a Russian princess, romance abounds in this necklace made with brass components, rosy crystals and a pendant. Add a pair of matching earrings for a beautiful set.

DESIGNS BY MOLLY SCHALLER

Skill Level: Easy

Materials

Stag ceramic pendant
8 (18mm) crystal copper Swarovski crystal rondelles
12 (3mm) Capri blue Swarovski crystal bicone beads
5 (8 x 12mm) peridot glass teardrop beads
2 (8mm) peridot Swarovski crystal margarita flower beads
30 (6 x 9mm) table-cut oval glass beads
4 brass flower pendant connectors
Brass filigree triangular-shaped component
11 (1-inch) brass eye pins
2 (2-inch) brass head pins
5 (8mm) brass jump rings
4 (2mm) brass crimp beads
2 brass ear wires
Brass hook-and-eye clasp
17½ inches 3mm brass cable chain
2 (7-inch) lengths .018-inch-diameter 7-strand gold nylon-coated flexible beading wire
Round-nose pliers
Chain-nose pliers
Wire nippers

Finished Sizes

Necklace
19½ inches (including clasp)
Earrings
1¼ inches long

Instructions

Necklace

1. Slide a Capri blue bicone bead, crystal copper rondelle and a Capri blue bicone bead on an eye pin; use round-nose pliers to form a loop after last bead. Trim excess wire. Repeat five additional times for a total of six beaded links.

2. To make the pendant, open a jump ring and slide on stag pendant; attach ring to centre top of filigree component as shown. Close ring. Attach the two remaining jump rings, one to each top corner of the filigree component.

3. Open a loop on a beaded link from step 1 and connect to one of the corner jump rings connected to filigree component; close loop. Open other loop on beaded link and connect to a flower pendant connector; close loop. In the same manner, attach the following to same side of necklace: beaded link, flower connector and a beaded link.

4. Repeat step 3 on other side of filigree connector.

5. String a crimp bead ½ inch from end of one 7-inch wire; thread short wire tail through last loop on a beaded link and back through crimp bead. Use crimp pliers to flatten and fold the crimp bead.

6. String 15 oval glass beads.

7. String a crimp bead; thread wire through a jump ring and back through crimp bead. Flatten and fold the crimp bead. Trim excess wire.

CONTINUED ON PAGE 116

Rainforest Jasper

These beautiful beads are all natural! The copper beads contrast with the lush green of the jasper for a very rich-looking set.

DESIGNS BY CAROLE RODGERS

Skill Level: Easy

Materials

50 x 43mm rainforest jasper pendant with large hole
Rainforest jasper flat beads: 18 (20 x 15mm) ovals, 22 (14 x 10mm) rectangles
20 (6.5 x 3.5mm) twisted copper metal tube beads
26 (3.5 x 6mm) copper fluted bicone beads
Copper round beads: 102 (3mm), 20 (2mm)
2 (4mm) copper jump rings
2 (2-inch) copper head pins
3 (1.3mm) copper crimp tubes
2 copper ear wires
Copper toggle clasp
2 (30-inch) lengths satin copper .015-inch-diameter 19-strand nylon-coated flexible beading wire
Round-nose pliers
Chain-nose pliers
Crimp pliers
Wire nippers
Tape

Finished Sizes

Necklace
22½ inches (including clasp)
Earrings
2⅛ inches long

Instructions

Necklace

1. Attach a piece of tape to a 30-inch wire 3 inches from one end.

2. String a 3mm copper round, copper fluted bicone, 3mm copper round and a rainforest jasper oval. Repeat eight additional times.

3. String a 3mm copper round, copper fluted bicone, 3mm copper round and a 2mm copper round.

4. String a copper fluted bicone. String a 2mm copper round and a 3mm copper round; repeat six additional times. String a 2mm copper round.

5. Insert wire through pendant and back through the last copper fluted bicone, forming a beaded loop.

6. String a 2mm copper round, twisted copper tube, 3mm copper round and a rainforest jasper rectangle. Repeat nine additional times, using 3mm copper rounds in place of 2mm copper

CONTINUED ON PAGE 116

Linked to Earth

Look luminescent in this set of pearls tucked among bayong wooden discs and cinnamon coral beads.

DESIGNS BY KATIE LEEDY

Skill Level: Intermediate

Materials

12 (15mm) tiger's-eye wooden flat round beads
7 (6–7mm) bayong wooden round beads
5 (5 x 14mm) gold mother-of-pearl tubes
25 (3 x 5mm) brown rondelle pearls
15 (3 x 7mm) coral rondelle beads
16 (6mm) sterling silver braided closed jump rings
7mm sterling silver closed jump ring
30 (2-inch) 24-gauge sterling silver head pins
2 (2 x 2mm) sterling silver crimp tubes
2 sterling silver ear wires
Sterling silver clasps: lobster-claw, "S"
12 inches 24-gauge sterling silver wire
16 inches sterling silver linked chain
12 inches .018-inch-diameter nylon-coated
    flexible beading wire
Round-nose pliers
Chain-nose pliers
Crimp pliers
Wire nippers

Finished Sizes
Necklace
17⅜ inches (including clasp)
Bracelet
7¼ inches (including clasp)
Earrings
2¼ inches long

Instructions
Necklace
1. Slide three coral rondelles onto a head pin; use round-nose pliers to form a wrapped head-pin loop above top rondelle. Trim excess wire.
2. Repeat step 1, substituting one pearl for three coral rondelles. Repeat three additional times.
3. Repeat step 1, substituting one mother-of-pearl tube for three coral rondelles. Repeat twice.
4. Repeat step 1, substituting one bayong wooden bead for three coral rondelles. Repeat three additional times.
5. Repeat step 1, substituting one tiger's-eye wooden flat bead for three coral rondelles. Repeat twice.
6. Repeat step 1, substituting one coral rondelle for three coral rondelles. Repeat once.
7. Repeat step 1, substituting a pearl and a coral rondelle for three coral rondelles. Repeat once.
8. Repeat step 1, substituting two coral rondelles for three coral rondelles.
9. Open a braided jump ring and slide on two beaded head pins that do not match; close ring. Repeat nine additional times, placing two beaded head pins on each jump ring.
10. Slide jump rings onto sterling silver chain in desired order.
11. Cut a 3-inch length of 24-gauge wire; form a wrapped loop ½ inch from one end of wire, attaching loop to end link on chain before wrapping. Slide a pearl onto wire and form another wrapped loop. Trim excess wire.

12. Repeat step 11 to opposite end of necklace. Slide "S" clasp onto one of the wire-wrapped loops; push side of clasp closed.

Bracelet

1. Repeat step 1 of necklace, substituting a bayong wooden bead for three coral rondelles. Repeat twice.

2. Repeat step 1 of necklace, substituting a mother-of-pearl tube for three coral rondelles. Repeat once.

3. Repeat step 1 of necklace, substituting a coral rondelle for three coral rondelles. Repeat once.

4. Repeat step 1 of necklace, substituting a pearl for three coral rondelles.

5. Open a braided jump ring and slide on two beaded head pins that do not match; close ring. Repeat three additional times.

6. String a crimp tube on beading wire ½ inch from one end; place wire end through lobster-claw clasp and back through crimp bead. Use crimp pliers to flatten the crimp bead.

7. String a tiger's-eye wooden flat bead, pearl, jump ring (from step 5. and a pearl.

8. String a tiger's-eye wooden flat bead, pearl, coral rondelle and a pearl.

9. Repeat step 7 twice; repeat step 8. Repeat step 7. String a tiger's-eye wooden flat bead.

10. String a crimp bead; place wire end through closed jump ring and back through crimp bead and several other beads. Flatten the crimp bead. Trim excess wire.

Earrings

1. Cut a 3-inch length of 26-gauge wire and form a wrapped loop ½ inch from one end. String a pearl, coral rondelle and a pearl. Form another wrapped loop; trim excess wire. Open loop on ear wire and slide on beaded wire; close loop.

2. Slide a tiger's-eye wooden flat bead on a head pin; form a wrapped head-pin loop above bead. Trim excess wire. Open a braided jump ring and slide on beaded head pin; attach ring to bottom loop of beaded wire. Close loop.

3. Repeat steps 1 and 2 for a second earring. ■

SOURCE: All materials from Gahanna Bead Shop.

Earthy Chic

Turquoise-glazed beads accentuate this set that pairs equally well with a T-shirt or an early autumn sweater set.

DESIGNS BY KAREN GALBRAITH

Skill Level: Intermediate

Materials
13 (13mm) turquoise round flat ceramic beads
20-gauge gunmetal wire: 15 (3-inch) lengths,
    14 (4-inch) lengths, 2 (2½-inch) lengths
Black permanent marker (optional)
Round-nose pliers
Chain-nose pliers
Nylon pliers
Wire nippers

Finished Sizes
Necklace
18½ inches (including clasp)
Earrings
2 inches long

Instructions
Necklace
1. Place one end of a 3-inch wire in jaws of round-nose pliers one fouth of the way up from widest part of the jaws; form a loop with wire end so wire forms a "p." Place pliers next to loop and wrap wire again, forming a second loop next to first one. Wire should look like the letter "B" with wire tail extending from back of letter. Reposition pliers in spot used for second loop and create third and fourth loops, creating a flower link (refer to Flower Link diagram). Repeat 13 additional times for a total of 14 flower links.

2. Use round-nose pliers to form a wrapped loop at one end of a 4-inch wire; string a ceramic bead. Form another wrapped loop. Trim excess wire. Repeat for each ceramic bead to form bead components.
3. Open a loop on a flower link and attach to a bead component; close loop. In the same manner, continue attaching flower links and bead components, alternating the two until there are two flower links and two bead components remaining. These will be used for the earrings.
4. For hook half of clasp, form a wrapped loop at one end of remaining 3-inch wire. Referring to Hook diagram, use largest part of round-nose pliers to bend wire into a hook shape. Create a small loop at end of wire hook. Open loop on last flower link on necklace and slide on hook; close loop.
5. For eye half of clasp, begin to form a wrapped loop at one end of remaining 4-inch wire, only do not wrap loop yet. Referring to Eye diagram, form a large loop. Hold end of wire tightly against wire loop and proceed to wrap wire tail around wire end, holding both wires together tightly. Trim excess wire. Attach to opposite end of necklace.
6. One at a time, place each flower link in jaws of nylon pliers and firmly but gently squeeze flowers; this will flatten and harden the flower links. Repeat with both halves of clasp.

Earrings

1. For ear wires, form a small loop at one end of a 2½-inch wire. Referring to Ear Wire diagram, form wire into an ear-wire shape. Repeat with other 2½-inch wire.

2. Open loops on ear wires and attach a bead component; close loops. Attach a flower link to the bottom of each bead component. ■

SOURCES: Wire from Artistic Wire; ceramic beads from Oriental Trading Co.

Flower Link

Hook

Eye

Ear Wire

Chic & Easy "Y" Necklace

Vibrant Czech glass beads and metal components make this a unique piece that's as versatile as it is beautiful.

DESIGN BY MARGOT POTTER

Skill Level: Easy

Materials
Czech glass beads: 18 (2 x 3mm) jet black/silver
   rondelle, 14 (8mm) turquoise faceted flat oval,
   15 (9 x 7mm) light olive green flat oval,
   1 (15 x 20mm) frosted clear leaf
12 (9mm) silver plastic saucer spacer beads
2 sterling silver jump rings
6 (22-gauge) sterling silver head pins
4 silver crimp tubes
2-into-1 sterling silver earring component
Silver square toggle clasp
2 (10-inch) lengths .018-inch-diameter
   nylon-coated flexible beading wire
Bead board (optional)
Round-nose pliers
Chain-nose pliers
Flush cutters

Finished Size
15 inches (including clasp), plus a 4-inch droplet

Instructions
Centre Droplet
1. Slide frosted clear leaf bead on a head pin; use round-nose pliers to form a wrapped head-pin loop above bead.
2. Cut off stopper from another head pin and use round-nose pliers to form end into a loop, forming an eye pin; slide on a silver saucer. Form another loop above saucer; trim excess wire. Set aside. Repeat once.

3. Repeat step 2 twice, substituting turquoise faceted flat ovals in place of silver saucer.
4. Repeat step 2, substituting a light olive green flat oval in place of silver saucer.
5. Open a loop on a beaded eye pin from step 2 and slide it onto bottom loop of earring component; close loop.
6. Open remaining loop on beaded eye pin and slide on a beaded eye pin from step 3; close loop. In the same manner, connect remaining beaded eye pins in the following order: light olive green flat oval, turquoise faceted flat oval and silver saucer. Use chain-nose pliers to secure loops closed.

7. Open bottom loop on last eye pin and slide on leaf pendant; close loop. Open a jump ring and slide it onto a top loop on earring component; close ring. Repeat to attach a jump ring to the other top loop on earring component. Set centre droplet aside.

Necklace
1. Cut a 10-inch length of beading wire. String a crimp tube onto one end of wire ½ inch from end; place wire end through one of the jump rings attached to centre droplet and back through crimp tube. Use chain-nose pliers to flatten and fold the crimp tube.
2. String a jet black/silver rondelle and a light olive green flat oval.
3. String the following: silver saucer, turquoise faceted flat oval, jet black/silver rondelle, light olive green flat oval, jet black/silver rondelle, turquoise faceted flat oval, silver saucer, light olive green flat oval, jet black/silver rondelle, turquoise faceted flat oval, jet black/silver rondelle and a light olive green flat oval; repeat once. String a silver saucer.
4. String a crimp tube and one half of clasp; place wire end back through crimp tube. Use chain-nose pliers to flatten and fold the crimp tube. Trim excess wire.
5. Repeat steps 1–4 to complete remaining half of necklace, attaching it to opposite top loop on earring component. ■

SOURCES: Czech glass beads from York Novelty Import Co.; plastic saucer beads from Great Craft Works; earring component from Fire Mountain Gems and Beads; clasp from Blue Moon Beads; findings from Marvin Schwab/The Bead Warehouse, beading wire from Beadalon.

Stone Filigree

There is no law that says filigree has to be metal! This carved-stone wonder gives you the look of filigree with an unusual twist.

DESIGN BY LAURIE D'AMBROSIO

Skill Level: Intermediate

Materials
3 carved red jade stations
Round beads: 9 (10mm) red jade,
   10 (6mm) red agate
43–44 inches carnelian chips
Approximately 160 tan or brown seed beads
Gold crimp tubes: 4 (.8mm),
   4 (1.3mm), 5 (1.5mm)
10mm or larger gold toggle clasp
120 inches .015-inch-diameter 7-strand
   nylon-coated flexible beading wire
Crimp pliers
Mini crimp pliers
Wire nippers
Tape

Finished Size
22¾ inches (including clasp), plus a 4-inch droplet

Project notes: *Tape ends of wires not being strung to keep beads from falling off. Use mini crimp pliers to crimp .8mm crimp tubes; use regular crimp pliers to crimp other crimp tubes.*

Instructions
1. Cut a 20-inch length of beading wire. Centre a hole at narrow end of a jade station on the wire. Hold both sides of wire together and string a 1.3mm crimp tube, positioning crimp tube next to jade station. Use crimp pliers to flatten and fold the crimp tube.

2. With wires together, string a red jade bead. Separate wires and randomly string 4 inches of carnelian chips and seed beads on each wire.
3. Hold wires together and string a red jade bead and five red agate beads.
4. With wires together, string a 1.3mm crimp tube; thread wire ends through one half of clasp and back through crimp tube and a red agate bead. Flatten and fold the crimp tube. Trim excess wire.
5. Repeat steps 1–4.
6. Cut two 14-inch lengths of wire. Thread both wires through opposite hole in narrow end of a previous jade station, centring the station on wires. Hold both sides of wires together and string a 1.5mm crimp tube, positioning the crimp tube next to the jade station. Flatten and fold the crimp tube. String a red jade bead.
7. Separate wires and randomly string 2½ inches of carnelian chips and seed beads on each wire.
8. Hold all four wires together and string a red jade bead. String a 1.5mm crimp tube; insert wires through hole in narrow end of remaining jade station and then back through crimp tube and red jade bead. Flatten and fold the crimp tube. Trim excess wire.
9. Repeat steps 6–8 to attach other side of necklace to centre jade station, referring to photo.
10. Cut two 12-inch lengths of wire. Thread wires through opposite narrow-end hole of centre jade station, centring wires. Hold all four wires together and string a 1.5mm crimp tube,

CONTINUED ON PAGE 117

Redefined Glamour

A spare pair of earrings makes a great necklace pendant.

DESIGN BY KRISTINE M. FRYE

Skill Level: Easy

Materials
20 fluorite chips
Smoky quartz beads: 2 (8 x 12mm), 2 (12 x 20mm)
Large earring or pendant that coordinates
    with beads
Silver jump rings: 2 (6mm), 17 (2mm)
8 silver eye pins
Silver lobster-claw clasp
10¾ inches 2mm silver Figaro chain
Round-nose pliers
2 pairs of chain-nose pliers
Wire nippers

Finished Size
20¾ inches (including clasp)

Instructions
1. Cut chain into eight 1-inch lengths and one 2¾-inch length.
2. String a smoky quartz bead on an eye pin; use round-nose pliers to form a loop after bead. Trim excess wire. Repeat for each smoky quartz bead.
3. String five fluorite chips on an eye pin; form a loop after last chip. Trim excess wire. Repeat three additional times.
4. Use both pairs of chain-nose pliers to open a 6mm jump ring; attach jump ring to end link of a 1-inch chain. Close jump ring.
5. Open a 2mm jump ring and attach to opposite end link and a fluorite eye pin; close ring.

6. In the same manner, use 2mm jump rings to continue attaching eye pins and chains together in the following order: 1-inch chain, 12 x 20mm smoky quartz, 1-inch chain, fluorite chips, 1-inch chain, 8 x 12mm smoky quartz, 2¾-inch chain, 8 x 12mm smoky quartz, 1-inch chain, fluorite chips, 1-inch chain, 12 x 20mm smoky quartz, 1-inch chain, fluorite chips and 1-inch chain.
7. Open another 2mm jump ring and slide on clasp; attach ring to end link of last chain.
8. If using an earring, remove it from ear wire. Open a 6mm jump ring and slide on earring or pendant; attach jump ring to centre link of necklace. ■

SOURCES: Fluorite chips and chain from Hobby Lobby Stores Inc.; similar smoky quartz beads found at Fire Mountain Gems and Beads.

Reticulating Clay Necklace

Polymer tiles and jump rings make a stunning centrepiece that moves with you when you wear it.

DESIGN BY MICHELLE HERREN

Skill Level: Intermediate

Materials

96 multicoloured E beads

32 (5–6mm) blackstone nugget beads

15 (4–5mm) silver Bali-style spacer beads

9 (6mm) silver jump rings

2 (1.3mm) silver crimp beads

Silver magnetic clasp

18 inches .018-inch-diameter nylon-coated flexible beading wire

¼ package black soft polymer clay

Pigment powders: gold, green, blue, purple

Watermark ink pad

Smooth ceramic tile

Clay machine or craft-dedicated pasta machine (optional)

⅜-inch square cutter

Paintbrush

Clay roller

Rotary drill with ¹⁄₁₆-inch drill bit or pin vice

Round-nose pliers

Flat-nose pliers

Crimp pliers

Wire nippers

Finished Size

19½ inches (including clasp)

Instructions

Clay Pendant

Project note: *Condition all clay by running it through clay machine 20–30 times, or knead with hands until clay is warm and pliable.*

1. Roll out clay using thickest setting on clay machine or by hand to ⅛ inch thick.

2. Lay clay on ceramic tile. Inking directly to clay, apply watermark ink liberally to clay.

3. Lightly dip paintbrush into a pigment powder, and in a circular motion, brush powder on clay, beginning in one corner, continuing until a small section of clay is covered. The area covered with powder should be large enough to cut two ⅜-inch squares from.

4. Repeat step 3 for each colour of pigment powder, making sure to overlap colours where they meet. The clay piece should look like a patchwork of colours when finished.

5. Use a square cutter to cut 6 squares, cutting at least one from each colour. Bake clay squares in oven at 265 degrees Fahrenheit for 30 minutes. Let pieces cool completely.

6. Position squares as shown in Fig. 1 and use drill to make holes where indicated.

7. Use jump rings to connect squares together. Attach jump rings through top holes; these two rings will be used to connect pendant to necklace.

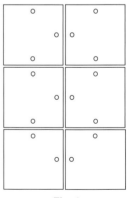

Fig. 1

Necklace

1. String a crimp bead ½ inch from one end of beading wire; place wire end through one half of clasp and back through crimp bead. Use crimp pliers to flatten and fold the crimp bead.

CONTINUED ON PAGE 117

Wild Rock

Don't leave out your favourite guy. Make this masculine necklace that features an assortment of wooden beads, bone and unusual mud beads from Africa for your favourite surfer boy.

DESIGN BY NEALAY PATEL

Skill Level: Beginner

Materials
2 (1-inch) black wooden cylinder tubes
8 (½-inch) faceted bone beads
4 (6–7mm) black wooden round beads
16 (½-inch) cone-shaped mud beads
3 (1-inch) black wooden faceted beads
4 (8/0) black seed beads
2 (1.3mm) silver crimp beads
Nickel-plated split ring
Nickel-plated lobster-claw clasp
20 inches .018-inch-diameter nylon-coated flexible
    beading wire
Round-nose pliers
Chain-nose pliers
Crimp pliers
Wire nippers

Finished Size
15⅝ inches (including clasp)

Instructions
1. String a crimp bead onto wire 1 inch from one end; place short wire tail through two black seed beads, clasp and back through seed beads and crimp bead. Use crimp pliers to flatten the crimp bead.
2. String the following: wooden tube, cone-shaped mud bead, faceted bone bead, cone-shaped mud

bead, faceted bone bead, cone-shaped mud bead, black round bead, cone-shaped mud bead, faceted bone bead, cone-shaped mud bead, black faceted wooden bead, cone-shaped mud bead, black round bead, cone-shaped mud bead, faceted bone bead and cone-shaped mud bead.
3. String black faceted wooden bead. Repeat step 2 in reverse to complete other half of necklace.
4. String a crimp bead, two black seed beads and split ring; place wire tail back through seed beads and crimp bead. Flatten the crimp bead. Trim excess wire. ■

SOURCE: Beads used on sample necklace are African trade beads and exact replicas may be difficult to find. Similar beads can be found on the Internet or from Fire Mountain Gems and Beads.

Copper Treats

Have you ever purchased a package of findings to make a pair of earrings and wondered what to do with the remaining findings? Why not make more earrings? These three pairs use the same findings, but keep the designs fresh by changing how they're used.

DESIGNS BY CAROLE RODGERS

Pair No. 1

Skill Level: Intermediate

Materials
2 (12mm) lampwork glass
   round beads
Copper beads: 4 (8mm)
   textured round, 14 (3mm)
   round, 2 (6mm) bicone,
   2 (4 x 6mm) spacers
6 (2-inch) copper head pins
2 (3-into-1. copper end connectors
2 (5mm) copper jump rings
2 copper ear wires
Round-nose pliers
Chain-nose pliers
Wire nippers

Finished Size
2½ inches long

Instructions
1. Slide the following on a head pin: 3mm round bead, 8mm textured round bead and a 3mm round bead. Use round-nose pliers to form a wrapped head-pin loop above top bead, attaching loop to a side loop on an end connector before wrapping.

Trim excess wire. Repeat to attach another beaded head pin to opposite side loop.
2. Slide the following on a head pin: 3mm round bead, lampwork bead, spacer bead, 3mm round bead, bicone bead and a 3mm round bead. In the same manner as in step 1, attach to centre loop of end connector between side loops.
3. Open a jump ring and attach to top loop on end connector; attach ring to ear wire. Close ring.
4. Repeat steps 1–3 for second earring.

Pair No. 2

Skill Level: Intermediate

Materials
Copper beads: 2 (8mm) textured round, 4 (3mm)
   round, 2 (6mm) bicone, 4 (6mm) fluted
2 (2-inch) copper head pins
2 (3-into-1. copper end connectors
6 (5mm) copper jump rings
2 copper ear wires
Round-nose pliers
Chain-nose pliers
Wire nippers

Finished Size
2⅝ inches long

Instructions

1. Slide the following on a head pin: 3mm round bead, bicone bead, fluted bead, 8mm textured round bead, fluted bead and a 3mm round bead. Form a wrapped head-pin loop above top bead; trim excess wire.

2. Open a jump ring and slide on beaded head pin; attach jump ring to single loop on an end connector; close ring.

3. Open two jump rings and attach one to each side loop on opposite side of end connector; attach both rings to ear wire. Close rings.

4. Repeat steps 1–3 for second earring.

Pair No. 3

Skill Level: Intermediate

Materials
Copper beads: 2 (10mm) round face,
  4 (6mm) bicone, 4 (3mm) round
2 (2-inch) copper head pins
4 (3-into-1. copper end connectors
8 (5mm) copper jump rings
2 copper ear wires

Round-nose pliers
Chain-nose pliers
Wire nippers

Finished Size
3 inches long

Instructions

1. Slide the following on a head pin: 3mm round bead, bicone bead, face bead, bicone bead and a 3mm round bead. Form a wrapped head-pin loop above top bead, attaching loop to single loop on an end connector before wrapping. Trim excess wire.

2. Attach a jump ring through each loop on 3-loop side of end connector; slide jump rings through holes on 3-loop side of another end connector. Close rings.

3. Open another jump ring and attach to top loop of previous end connector; attach ring to ear wire. Close ring.

4. Repeat steps 1–3 for second earring. ■

SOURCES: Copper end connectors from Cousin Corp. of America; jump rings from Beadalon.

Surprising Sequins

Sequins aren't just for crafting anymore! These stacked stunners have a whole new look.

DESIGN BY KRISTINE M. FRYE

Skill Level: Easy

Materials

1 package 8mm red sequins
12 (6mm) silver spacers
4 (4mm) Siam Swarovski crystal bicone beads
6 (5mm) silver jump rings
4 (2-inch) silver eye pins
4 silver head pins
2 silver ear wires
2¼ inches silver fine-link chain
Round-nose pliers
Chain-nose pliers
Wire nippers

Finished Size

3½ inches long

Instructions

1. Slide the following on an eye pin: silver spacer, ⅜ inch of sequins, silver spacer, ⅜ inch of sequins and a silver spacer. Form a wrapped loop after last spacer. Trim excess wire. Set aside. Repeat three additional times.

2. Cut chain into two ⅜-inch lengths and two ¾-inch lengths. Use a jump ring to attach a piece of chain to each eye pin.

3. Open a jump ring and slide on end links of a short and long chain; attach ring to ear wire. Close jump ring. Repeat for second earring.

4. Slide a bicone crystal onto a head pin; form a wrapped loop after crystal, attaching loop to bottom loop of an eye pin before wrapping. Trim excess wire. Repeat to attach a bicone crystal to each eye pin. ■

SOURCES: Chain from Blue Moon Beads; sequins from Westrim Crafts; silver spacers from Hobby Lobby Stores Inc.; jump rings, eye pins, head pins and ear wires from Bead Source Inc.; crystals from Swarovski North America.

Copper Rounds

Fashion your own copper rounds for these stunning disc earrings featuring Swarovski crystals.

DESIGN BY ANNE IGOU

Skill Level: Intermediate

Materials

Medium-weight copper soft metal sheet
Clear Swarovski crystal beads: 2 (12mm) bicone, 12 (7mm) cones
2 (2mm) copper round beads
12 (4mm) copper heishe beads
14 copper head pins
2 copper ear wires
Ammonia
Face mask
Airtight plastic container
Spray bottle
Paper towels
Circle cutters: ¾- and 2-inch
3-inch-square piece of felt
Steel bench block
Ball-peen hammer
Needle tool
Ball stylus
Round-nose pliers
Wire nippers
Scissors

Finished Size

2¾ inches long

Project note: *When working with ammonia, wear a face mask and work in a well-ventilated area to prevent exposure to chemical fumes.*

Instructions

1. Place a 5 x 3-inch piece of copper sheet into airtight plastic container; fill spray bottle with ammonia and spray a fine mist onto copper sheet. Seal container for one hour. Remove copper sheet and wipe off excess ammonia with paper towels.

2. Place felt on steel bench block; lay copper sheet on top of felt and hammer entire sheet until desired effect is achieved.

3. Place 2-inch circle cutter on top of copper sheet and trace around cutter, pressing into the copper with ball stylus. Cut out circle with scissors. Repeat to make another copper circle.

4. Place ¾-inch circle cutter on top of one cutout circle approximately ¼ inch from top. In the same manner as in step 3, trace and cut out circle, forming a hoop. Repeat for other copper circle.

5. Use needle tool to poke two small holes through a hoop, one positioned just above centre top of cutout circle and the other directly above first hole $\frac{1}{16}$ inch from top edge. Poke six additional holes along bottom edge of hoop $\frac{1}{8}$ inch from edge. Repeat for other hoop.

6. Slide a copper heishe bead and a clear cone bead on a head pin; use round-nose pliers to form a loop above top bead. Trim excess wire. Repeat 11 additional times.

7. Open loops on beaded head pins and attach to holes along bottom edge of hoops. Close loops.

8. Slide a clear bicone bead and a copper round bead on a head pin; form a loop above top bead. Trim excess wire. Open loop and attach to hole just above cutout circle, so head pin dangles in centre of hoop. Close loop. Repeat for other hoop.

9. Open loops on ear wires and attach to top holes on hoops; close loops. ■

SOURCES: Copper sheet from American Art Clay Co.; crystal beads, copper beads, ear wires and head pins from Jewelry Supply Inc.

Balancing Act

Spacer bars create earrings with the graceful movement of mobiles.

DESIGN BY MOLLY SCHALLER

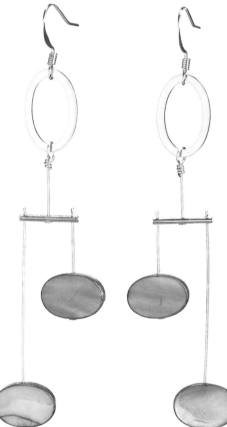

Skill Level: Intermediate

Materials
4 (½ x ⅜-inch) dyed shell oval beads
2 (13mm) gold 3-hole spacer bars
6 (2-inch) gold head pins
2 (12 x 18mm) gold solid oval rings
2 gold ear wires
Round-nose pliers
Chain-nose pliers
Wire nippers

Finished Size
3½ inches long

Instructions
1. Slide a shell oval on a head pin; thread head pin through a side hole of a spacer bar. Use chain-nose pliers to bend the very top of the head pin to secure it to spacer bar.
2. Slide a shell oval on a head pin; thread head pin through other side hole of same spacer bar. Cut off 1 inch from end of head pin and secure to spacer bar in the same manner as before.
3. Thread a head pin through centre hole of spacer bar so head is on same side as shell ovals; use round-nose pliers to form a wire-wrapped loop with head pin ½ inch above spacer bar, attaching loop to oval ring before wrapping. Trim excess wire.
4. Open loop on ear wire and attach to oval ring; close loop.
5. Repeat steps 1–4 for second earring. ■

Sources: Shell beads from Eclectica; spacer bars and oval rings from Beadalon.

Round & Round

Wrap precious coins around your wrist. This set takes mere minutes to make and will get noticed everywhere you go!

DESIGNS BY DIANNE DE VIENNE

Skill Level: Easy

Materials

8 (10mm) white freshwater pearl coins
9 (10mm) brushed gold vermeil coin-shaped beads
16 (3mm) gold vermeil Bali-style daisy spacers
2 (1.3mm) gold crimp beads
2 (1½-inch) gold-filled head pins
2 gold-filled ear wires
10mm gold vermeil toggle clasp
13 inches .018-inch-diameter nylon-coated flexible beading wire
Round-nose pliers
Chain-nose pliers
Wire nippers

Finished Sizes

Bracelet
7 inches (including clasp)

Earrings
1¾ inches long

Instructions

Bracelet

1. String a crimp bead on beading wire ½ inch from one end; place wire end through one half of clasp and back through crimp bead. Use chain-nose pliers to flatten and fold the crimp bead.

2. String four daisy spacers. String a gold vermeil coin and a pearl coin; repeat five additional times. String a gold vermeil coin and four daisy spacers.

3. String a crimp bead; place wire end through other half of clasp and back through crimp bead and gold vermeil coin. Gently pull wire taut. Flatten and fold the crimp bead; trim excess wire.

Earrings

Slide the following on a head pin: daisy spacer, pearl coin, gold vermeil coin and three daisy spacers. Use round-nose pliers to form a wrapped head-pin loop above top spacer, attaching loop to ear wire before wrapping. Trim excess wire. Repeat for second earring. ■

SOURCES: Pearl coins from BeadsWeb; gold vermeil coins, daisy spacers and clasp from You and Me Findings; head pins and ear wires from South Pacific Wholesale Co.

Spotlight Button Bracelet

Your favourite button takes centre stage among a dramatic jewel-tone mix of pearls and sparkling blue goldstone rounds.

DESIGN BY MICHELLE MACH

Skill Level: Beginner

Materials

8mm pearls: 9 green, 9 blue
4–5mm potato pearls: 10 black cherry, 16 iris blue, 14 iris green
13 (4mm) blue goldstone round beads
5 (6mm) grey Swarovski crystal pearls
4 (2mm) silver round beads
2 (2mm) silver crimp beads
¾-inch-diameter button
6mm silver jump ring
5mm silver spring-ring clasp
2 (9-inch) lengths .012-inch-diameter nylon-coated flexible beading wire
Crimp pliers
Wire nippers
Tape

Finished Size

8¼ inches (including clasp)

Instructions

1. Hold both wire lengths together and string a crimp bead ½ inch from one end; place wire ends through loop on spring-ring clasp and back through crimp bead. Use crimp pliers to flatten and fold the crimp bead.

2. Separate wires. String a silver round bead and a goldstone round bead on one wire. String 35–37 pearls and goldstone round beads in a random pattern. String a goldstone round bead and a silver round bead. Attach a piece of tape to end of wire.

3. Repeat step 2 with other wire.

4. Open jump ring and attach to button shank; close ring. *Note: If hole on button shank is large enough to accommodate clasp, this step may be skipped.*

5. Remove tape. Hold wires together and string a crimp bead; thread wire ends through jump ring and back through crimp bead and last goldstone round bead. *Note: If step 4 was skipped, attach wires to button shank instead.* Flatten and fold the crimp bead; trim excess wire. ■

SOURCES: Button from Jo-Ann Stores Inc.; all other materials from Fire Mountain Gems and Beads.

High Wattage Pearls

This eye-popping Swarovski clasp is just what the doctor ordered to ramp up your pearls for a special holiday bash.

DESIGN BY BRENDA MORRIS JARRETT

Skill Level: Intermediate

Materials

10 light orange nugget pearls

12 (7 x 5mm) copper top-drilled rice pearls

Sterling silver round beads: 4 (6mm), 24 (2mm)

Swarovski crystal beads: 5 (6mm) crystal copper rondelle, 8 (6mm) crystal copper round, 12 (6mm) topaz smoky AB bicone, 16 (4mm) topaz smoky AB bicone, 16 (4mm) crystal copper bicone

Sterling silver rondelle beads: 12 (5mm), 8 (4mm)

44 (8/0) matte brown AB seed beads

8 (1.5mm) sterling silver crimp beads

8 sterling silver crimp covers

24 x 16 x 11mm faceted domed copper Swarovski crystal magnetic clasp

4 (10-inch) lengths .018-inch-diameter 49-strand nylon-coated flexible beading wire

Crimp pliers

Wire nippers

Tape

Finished Size

8 inches (including clasp)

Instructions

1. String a crimp bead 1 inch from one end of a 10-inch wire; thread short wire tail through slot on top half of clasp (this will be the side with the crystal). Insert wire back through crimp bead. Use crimp pliers to flatten and fold the crimp bead.

2. String the following: crystal copper bicone, crystal copper rondelle, 4mm sterling silver rondelle, 6mm topaz smoky AB bicone, 5mm sterling silver rondelle, light orange nugget pearl, 5mm sterling silver rondelle, 6mm topaz smoky AB bicone, 6mm sterling silver round, crystal copper round and a light orange nugget pearl.

3. String a crystal copper round, 4mm sterling silver rondelle, 6mm topaz smoky AB bicone, 5mm sterling silver rondelle, light orange nugget pearl, 5mm sterling silver rondelle, 6mm topaz smoky AB bicone, 4mm sterling silver rondelle and a crystal copper round.

4. Repeat step 2, only in reverse.

5. String a crimp bead. Insert wire through one hole on bottom half of clasp and back through crimp bead and a few other beads. Use crimp pliers to flatten and fold the crimp bead. *Note: Check to see that bottom half of clasp is positioned to correctly fasten to top half before crimping the crimp bead. Trim excess wire.*

6. Repeat steps 1–5 to attach another 10-inch wire to clasp. These two strands will be the outside strands.

7. String a crimp bead, 4mm topaz smoky AB bicone and a seed bead on another 10-inch wire 1 inch from end; thread short wire tail through slot on top half of clasp between the outside strands and then back through the three beads. Flatten and fold the crimp bead.

8. String the following: crystal copper bicone, top-drilled rice pearl, seed bead, 4mm topaz smoky AB

bicone, 2mm sterling silver round, crystal copper bicone, top-drilled rice pearl and a seed bead.

9. Thread wire through the second 5mm sterling silver rondelle on outside strand (Fig. 1). Keeping wire outside of outside strand, string the following: 2 seed beads, 2mm sterling silver round, 2 seed beads, 2mm sterling silver round and 2 seed beads.

10. Thread wire back through to the inside through crystal copper round bead (Fig. 2).

11. String a 2mm sterling silver round, seed bead, 4mm topaz smoky AB bicone, 2mm sterling silver round, crystal copper bicone, top-drilled rice pearl, seed bead, 4mm topaz smoky AB bicone and a 2mm sterling silver round.

12. String a crystal copper rondelle.

13. Repeat step 11, only in reverse.

14. Thread wire through the last crystal copper round bead on the same outside strand.

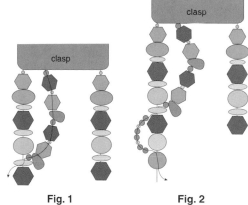

Fig. 1   Fig. 2

15. Keeping wire on the outside of the outside beaded strand, string beading sequence from step 9. Thread wire back through the next to last 5mm sterling silver rondelle. Repeat step 8, only in reverse.

CONTINUED ON PAGE 117

About Face Watch

Get out your rubber stamps to make stylish tile beads.

DESIGN BY MICHELLE HERREN

Materials

Silver watch face
7 (4mm) black cube beads
12 silver spacers
2 (1.3mm) silver crimp beads
20 inches elastic beading cord
Various rubber stamps
Ink pads: metallic gold pearlescent,
    black solvent-based
Pigment powders: dark gold, blue, gold,
    yellow, dark copper
Metallic pearl soft polymer clay
Smooth ceramic tile
½-inch-square cutter
Crimp pliers
Paintbrush
Texture tool such as an unused kitchen
    scrubbing pad
Rotary drill or pin vice with ¹⁄₁₆-inch drill bit
Clay machine or craft-dedicated pasta machine
    (optional)
Polymer clay sealant

Finished Size

8 inches

Project note: *Condition clay by running it through clay machine 20–30 times, or knead with hands until clay is warm and pliable.*

Instructions

1. Roll out clay using thickest setting on clay machine or by hand to ⅛ inch thick.

2. Use black solvent ink to ink only the portions of stamps that will be featured on clay squares; stamp images on clay. Use ½-inch-square cutter to cut six squares from stamped clay.

3. Place clay squares on ceramic tile. Lightly brush each square with one or more pigment powders.

4. Turn squares over and add texture with texture tool to the back of each. Inking directly to clay, apply metallic gold ink to the back of each square.

5. Following manufacturer's instructions, bake squares. Let cool completely before handling.

6. Use rotary tool or pin vice to drill two ¹⁄₁₆-inch holes all the way through each square; holes should be positioned approximately ⅛ inch in from sides.

7. Apply a light coat of clay sealant to the front of each square; this will create a shine and also lock in pigment powders. Let dry.

8. Fold beading cord in half; insert folded end through one loop on watch face, to make a lark's head knot (see General Instructions, page 8). Thread unfolded ends through loop formed by cord and pull gently, securing cord to watch loop. Hold cord strands together and string a crimp bead, placing it up against loop; use crimp pliers to flatten crimp bead in place.

9. With cords together, string a black cube bead and a silver spacer.

10. Separate cords and string both through

CONTINUED ON PAGE 117

On the Square

This stunning, up-to-date bracelet is easy to make!

DESIGN BY JEAN YATES

Skill Level: Beginner

Materials
11 (12mm) copper Swarovski crystal pearls
12 (4mm) crystal copper Swarovski crystal round beads
12 (8.7 x 8.8mm) antique copper-plated beaded square rings
2 (3mm) sterling silver crimp beads
23.4 x 23.8mm copper-plated hammered diamond toggle clasp
16 inches .019-inch-diameter nylon-coated flexible beading wire
Chain-nose pliers
Crimp pliers
Wire nippers

Finished Size
8½ inches (including clasp)

Instructions
1. String a crimp bead ½ inch from one end of beading wire; place short wire tail through one half of clasp and back through crimp bead. Use crimp pliers to flatten the crimp bead.

2. String a crystal copper round and a square ring. String a copper pearl, crystal copper round and a square ring; repeat 10 additional times. The square rings will move and sit on top of the crystal copper rounds.

3. String a crimp bead; place wire through remaining half of clasp and back through crimp bead and last crystal copper round. Flatten the crimp bead. Trim excess wire. ■

SOURCES: Swarovski crystal rounds, crystal pearls, square rings and toggle clasp from Fusion Beads; crimp beads from Via Murano.

Stag's Bride
Continued from page 82

8. Repeat steps 5–7 on other side of necklace.
9. Using chain-nose pliers, bend one eye pin at a 120-degree angle at base of eye (Fig. 1). Bend wire back so it is perpendicular to the eye into a hanger-like shape (Fig. 2). Slide a peridot teardrop bead onto wire and bend wire tail up toward the eye. Wrap wire tail around base of loop (Fig. 3). Trim excess wire. Repeat four additional times.
10. Determine centre of chain. Open loop on one teardrop droplet from step 9 and attach to centre chain link; close loop. Repeat to attach remaining teardrop droplets to chain every 1¼ inches, as shown.
11. Open jump rings at ends of necklace and attach ends of chain; slide one half of clasp on each end of necklace. Close jump rings.

Earrings
1. On a 2-inch head pin, slide a peridot margarita bead and a crystal copper rondelle. Use round-nose pliers to form a wrapped head-pin loop at top of wire. Trim excess wire.
2. Bend wire so it follows the contours of the

rondelle bead, positioning wrapped loop centred above rondelle as shown in photo.
3. Repeat steps 1 and 2.
4. Open loops on ear wires and attach wrapped loops; close loops.

SOURCES: Stag pendant from Lake Quinsigamond Pottery; brass findings, filigree and flower connectors from Vintaj Natural Brass Co.; glass teardrop and glass oval beads from Halcraft USA; crystals from Swarovski North America; beading wire from Beadalon.

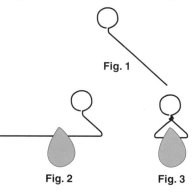

Fig. 1

Fig. 2   Fig. 3

Rainforest Jasper
Continued from page 84

round. String two 3mm copper rounds.
7. Carefully remove tape from wire and hold both wire ends together; thread wires through two crimp tubes. Insert wire ends through bar end of clasp and back through crimp tubes. Gently pull wire. Use crimp pliers to flatten and fold the crimp tubes; trim excess wire.

8. Repeat steps 1–7 for other side of necklace, only string one crimp tube instead of two.

Earrings
1. Slide a 3mm copper round, copper fluted bicone, rainforest jasper rectangle, copper fluted bicone and a 3mm copper round on a head pin; use round-nose pliers to form a wrapped head-pin loop above top bead. Trim excess wire. Repeat once.
2. Open jump rings and slide on beaded head pins; attach jump rings to ear wires. Close rings.

SOURCES: Head pins, jump rings, crimp tubes and beading wire from Beadalon. Similar beads can be found at Bead Trust.

Stone Filigree
Continued from page 92

positioning the crimp tube next to the jade station. Flatten and fold the crimp tube. String a red jade bead.
11. Separate wires. String 1 to 2 inches of carnelian chips and seed beads on each wire for random lengths. String a .8mm crimp tube after last bead on each wire. Pass wire ends around crimp tubes and back through a few beads. Flatten and fold the crimp tube for each wire. Trim excess wires. ■

SOURCES: Jade stations, red jade beads, red agate beads and carnelian chips from Fire Mountain Gems and Beads; crimp tubes and beading wire from Beadalon.

Reticulating Clay Necklace
Continued from page 96

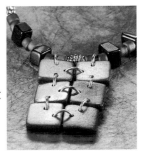

2. String two E beads and a nugget. String two E beads, a nugget, two E beads, silver spacer, two E beads and a nugget; repeat 14 additional times. String two E beads, a nugget and two E beads.
3. String a crimp bead; place wire end through remaining half of clasp and back through crimp bead. Flatten and fold the crimp bead. Trim excess wire.
4. Open jump rings at top of pendant and attach to centre of necklace. Close rings. ■

SOURCES: Blackstone nuggets from Expo International Inc.; E beads from Vegas Beads; clasp, beading wire, crimp beads, spacer beads and jump rings from Fire Mountain Gems and Beads; polymer clay from American Art Clay Co.; pigment powders from Jacquard Products; watermark ink pad from Tsukineko Inc.; square cutter from Kemper Enterprises Inc.; clay machine from Makin's Clay.

High Wattage Pearls
Continued from page 111

16. String a crimp bead, 4mm topaz smoky AB bicone and a seed bead. Attach tape to wire end.
17. Repeat steps 7–11 with remaining 10-inch wire, stringing wire through other outside wire.
18. String wire through the same crystal copper rondelle on which other strand is strung. Repeat steps 13–16.
19. Make sure all beads are snug against each other. Remove tape from one strand. Insert wire through a hole on bottom half of clasp and back through the last three beads, including the crimp bead. Flatten and fold the crimp bead. Repeat for remaining strand, attaching it to other hole on bottom half of clasp. Trim excess wire.
20) Use crimp pliers to secure crimp covers over crimp beads. ■

SOURCES: Clasp, Swarovski crystals, rice pearls and sterling silver round beads from Fire Mountain Gems and Beads; nugget pearls from Artbeads.com; beading wire from Beadalon.

About Face Watch
Continued from page 112

separate holes of a square tile. With cords together, string a silver spacer, black cube bead and a silver spacer.
11. Repeat step 10 five additional times, but do not string last silver spacer.
12. String a crimp bead; insert cords through empty loop on watch face and back through crimp bead. Flatten the crimp bead. Trim excess cord. ■

SOURCES: Watch face, black cube beads, silver spacers, crimp beads and elastic cord from Fire Mountain Gems and Beads; soft polymer clay from AMACO; pigment powders and pearlescent ink pad from Jacquard Products; solvent ink pad from Tsukineko Inc.; rubber stamps from Stampin' Up!, Inkadinkado and Stampers Anonymous; square cutter from Kemper Enterprises Inc.; clay machine from Makin's Clay; polymer clay sealant from Covered in Clay.

Cranberry Crush

Swarovski crystals and gold accents create jewellery that glitters!

DESIGNS BY DEBBIE TUTTLE

Skill Level: Easy

Materials

Red plastic round beads: 11 (6mm), 10 (8mm),
    4 (10mm), 2 (12mm)
Swarovski crystal round beads in varying shades of
    red: 12 (6mm), 2 (7mm), 26 (8mm), 2 (9mm),
    8 (10mm), 1 (14mm)
Swarovski crystal bicone beads in varying shades
    of red: 12 (4mm), 8 (6mm)
Red double crystal beads: 8 (10mm), 4 (12mm)
Gold flat spacers: 52 (3mm), 51 (5mm)
2 (16mm) gold separator bars with 3 holes
5mm gold soldered jump ring
5mm gold split ring
3 (1¼-inch) gold head pins
2 (1-inch) gold eye pins
4 (3mm) gold round beads
8 (2mm) gold twisted crimp beads
2 gold French ear wires
Gold 15mm toggle clasp
Gold 20mm 3-loop slider clasp
57 inches .015-inch-diameter nylon-coated flexible
    beading wire
Round-nose pliers
Chain-nose pliers
Crimp pliers
Wire nippers
Tape

Finished Sizes

Necklace
18 inches (including clasp)

Bracelet
7¼ inches (including clasp)

Earrings
2 inches long

Instructions

Necklace

1. Cut a 24-inch length of beading wire. String a crimp bead ½ inch from one end of wire; place short wire tail through one half of toggle clasp and back through crimp bead. Use crimp pliers to flatten the crimp bead.

2. String two gold round beads. String the following, stringing a 5mm gold spacer after each: 6mm plastic, 6mm round, 7mm round, 8mm round, 8mm plastic, 8mm round, 8mm plastic, 8mm round, 8mm plastic, 8mm round, 10mm plastic, 10mm round, 10mm double crystal, two 10mm round, 12mm double crystal, 12mm plastic, 12mm double crystal and a 10mm double crystal.

3. String a 14mm round and a 5mm spacer. Beginning with a 10mm double crystal, repeat step 2, only in reverse, to string the remaining half of the necklace.

4. String a crimp bead; thread wire through other half of clasp and back through crimp bead. Flatten the crimp bead; trim excess wire.

5. Slide a 10mm round, 5mm gold spacer and a 6mm plastic bead on a head pin; form a loop above top bead. Trim excess wire. Open loop and attach to jump ring; close loop. Attach jump ring to split ring; attach split ring to round end of clasp.

Bracelet

1. Cut three 11-inch lengths of beading wire.

2. String a crimp bead ½ inch from one end of one wire; thread short wire tail through one of the side loops on one half of slide clasp and back through crimp bead. Flatten the crimp bead.

3. String the following: 4mm bicone, 3mm spacer, 6mm round, 3mm spacer, 6mm bicone, 3mm spacer, 8mm round, 3mm spacer and a 4mm bicone.

4. Insert wire through a side hole of a separator bar.

5. String a 4mm bicone, 8mm round, 3mm spacer, 6mm bicone, 3mm spacer, 8mm round, 3mm spacer, 6mm plastic, 3mm spacer, 8mm round, 3mm spacer, 6mm plastic, 3mm spacer, 8mm round, 3mm spacer, 6mm plastic, 3mm spacer, 8mm round, 3mm spacer, 6mm bicone, 3mm spacer, 8mm round and a 4mm bicone. Repeat step 4 with another separator bar.

6. Repeat step 3, only in reverse. String a crimp bead. Attach tape to wire end.

CONTINUED ON PAGE 152

After Midnight

Brown, burgundy, bronze and rose crystal pearls in this stunning choker and earring set are the picture of sophistication when accented by glass window beads and blushing seed beads.

DESIGNS BY MOLLY SCHALLER

Skill Level: Intermediate

Materials
Swarovski crystal pearls:
   41 (12mm) mix of brown, burgundy and powder rose, 26 (8mm) mix of brown, burgundy, powder rose and bronze, 25 (6mm) mix of burgundy and bronze, 12 (4mm) powder rose
16 (4mm) burgundy crystal round beads
10 (12mm) pink glass table-cut square window beads
129 blush seed beads
6 silver crimp tubes
6 (1-inch) sterling silver ball-tipped head pins
2 sterling silver French ear wires
Silver magnetic pumpkin leaf clasp
2 (2-inch) lengths 24-gauge silver half-hard wire
3 (20-inch) lengths .019-inch-diameter 49-strand nylon-coated flexible beading wire
Round-nose pliers
Chain-nose pliers
Crimp pliers
Flush cutters

Finished Sizes
Choker
17½ inches (including clasp)
Earrings
2⅛ inches long

Instructions
Choker
1. String a crimp tube on one 20-inch wire ½ inch from end; place short wire tail through side loop on one half of clasp and back through crimp tube. Use crimp pliers to flatten and fold the crimp tube.
2. Beginning with a seed bead, string 31 seed beads and 30 (12mm) pearls, alternating between the two. Strand should measure approximately 16 inches.
3. String a crimp tube; insert wire through opposite side loop on other half of clasp and back through crimp tube and one seed bead.
Note: *If wire was first strung through the left-side loop, then wire will be strung through right-side loop and vice versa. This will provide a twist in the necklace.* Flatten and fold the crimp tube. Trim excess wire.
4. Repeat step 1 to attach a 20-inch wire to centre loop of clasp.
5. Set aside the following: two 8mm bronze pearls, two burgundy crystals, two 4mm powder rose pearls and two window beads. These will be used for the earrings.
6. String pearls and all remaining window beads, stringing a seed bead between each. Continue stringing until strand measures approximately 16 inches. The strand should begin and end with a seed bead and all the window beads and 12mm pearls should be strung.

7. Repeat step 3 to attach wire to centre loop on other half of clasp.

8. Repeat step 1 to attach remaining 20-inch wire to last side loop of clasp.

9. String remaining pearls and crystals, stringing a seed bead between each until strand measures approximately 16 inches. Strand should begin and end with a seed bead.

10. Repeat step 3 to attach wire to opposite side loop on other half of clasp.

Earrings

1. Use round-nose pliers to form a wrapped loop ½ inch from one end of a 2-inch wire. String a seed bead, window bead and a seed bead. Form a wrapped loop above seed bead; trim excess wire. Repeat once. Open loops on ear wires and slide on beaded wires; close loops.

2. Slide a burgundy crystal on a head pin; form a loop above crystal. Trim excess wire. Repeat for each remaining pearl and crystal.

3. Open loops of beaded head pins and attach one of each kind to bottom loop below window beads; close loops. ■

SOURCES: Crystals and crystal pearls from Swarovski North America; glass window beads from Halcraft USA; seed beads, crimp beads and beading wire from Beadalon; sterling silver ear wires from Blue Moon Beads; magnetic clasp from HandFast.

Crystal Midnight

Dramatic and demure at the same time, this necklace provides a great opportunity to practice knotting, and you'll love this timeless set for years to come.

DESIGNS BY MOLLY SCHALLER

Skill Level: Easy

Materials
54 (5–6mm) jet Swarovski crystal round beads
22 (11 x 10mm) jet Swarovski crystal flat briolettes
5 (9 x 5mm) jet Swarovski crystal briolette pendants
5 silver jump rings
2 silver ear wires
4 (¼-inch) lengths silver French wire
Silver lobster-claw clasp
2 inches silver cable chain
Size 4 black silk beading cord, with attached needle
Knotting tool
Wire nippers
Jewellery cement

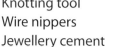

Finished Sizes
Necklace
16¼ inches (including clasp), plus a 2-inch extender
Earrings
2 inches long

Instructions
Necklace
1. Remove silk cord from card and gently stretch it until all kinks are removed; tie a knot 1 inch from end.

2. String three crystal round beads, one length of French wire and clasp. Thread the needle back through the first bead, turning the French wire into a loop attaching the clasp.

3. Make a knot by hand, positioning it snugly against the bead. Pass needle through next bead and repeat knot. Place a drop of glue on this knot and pass needle through next crystal.

4. Use the knotting tool to make a knot after the third crystal. Trim the tail end of the silk cord, leaving the needle end connected.

5. String 15 crystal round beads, using the knotting tool to knot after each bead.

6. String four flat briolettes; pass needle back through the first two briolettes, in the same direction, forming a shamrock shape. Make sure these beads are close to the previous knot. Make another knot with the knotting tool, securing shamrock shape of beads in place. String three more crystal round beads, knotting after each bead.

7. Repeat step 6 four additional times.

8. String 12 crystal round beads, knotting after each bead. String three more crystal round beads, one length of French wire and end link of chain. Insert needle back through the last three beads, forming a loop with French wire. Knot the last three beads by hand in the same manner as in steps 2-4. Place a drop of glue on last knot; trim excess cord.

9. Open a jump ring and slide on a pendant briolette; attach to end link of chain. Close jump ring. Repeat four more times, attaching jump rings to every other link of chain.

Earrings

1. Tie a knot at end of remaining silk cord and string three crystal round beads and a flat briolette.
2. Leaving 1 inch of cord between briolette and crystal round beads, tie a square knot snugly above the point of the briolette.

3. Pass the needle back through all three crystal round beads. String one length of French wire and pass the needle back through the crystal round bead closest to the French wire. Finish in the same manner as in steps 3 and 4 of the necklace. Trim excess cord.
4. Slide French wire loop onto open ear-wire loop. Close ear-wire loop.
5. Repeat steps 1–4 for second earring. ■

SOURCES: Crystals from Swarovski North America; silk cord, clasp, French wire, jewellery cement and knotting tool from Beadalon; chain from Blue Moon Beads.

Porcelain Couture

Old becomes new again when a deconstructed vintage necklace is transformed into this tasselled trio.

DESIGNS BY CANDIE COOPER

Skill Level: Intermediate

Materials

Blue and white ceramic beads: 1 (30mm) oval,
  1 (25mm) oval, 4 (10mm) round, 4 (12mm) round
2 (9–10mm) blue round beads
15 (5mm) cobalt blue round glass beads
Gold round beads: 8 (4mm) smooth,
  1 (6mm) corrugated
Gold bead caps: 2 (9mm), 21 (5mm)
8mm gold jump ring
Gold chain tassels: 1½-inch, 3¼-inch with 14mm
  gold corrugated round bead
3 (2-inch) gold head pins
Gold eye pin
2 (1.5mm) gold crimp beads
2 gold ear wires with long shanks
16.8mm gold toggle clasp
21 inches gold chain with clasp
12 inches .018-inch-diameter 49-strand
  nylon-coated flexible beading wire
Round-nose pliers
Flat-nose pliers
Crimp pliers
Wire nippers
Vintage necklace components were used to make
  sample pieces.

Finished Sizes

Necklace
21½ inches (including clasp), plus a 4½-inch droplet

Bracelet
8⅛ inches (including clasp)
Earrings
1⅜ inches long

Instructions

Necklace

1. Slide a 9mm bead cap, 30mm blue and white ceramic oval bead and a 9mm bead cap on an eye pin; use round-nose pliers to form a loop above bead cap. Trim excess wire. Open bottom loop and attach to 3¼-inch chain tassel; close loop. This will be the centre dangle.

2. Open jump ring and slide on top loop of centre dangle; close jump ring. Slide jump ring on gold chain.

3. Slide a 5mm bead cap, 10mm blue and white ceramic round bead, 5mm bead cap, cobalt blue round bead and a 5mm bead cap on a head pin; form a loop above top bead cap. Trim excess wire. Open loop and attach to clasp end of chain; close loop.

Bracelet

1. Use pliers to open loop at top of 1½-inch chain tassel and remove any beads above chain; do not remove bead cap covering chains. String a 10mm blue and white ceramic round bead and a gold corrugated round bead. Form a loop above top bead; trim excess wire.

2. String a crimp bead on wire ½ inch from one

CONTINUED ON PAGE 153

Satin Doll

Black Swarovski crystals and cathedral-cut glass beads add a touch of midnight sparkle to this set that will complement your favourite little black dress.

DESIGNS BY MOLLY SCHALLER

Skill Level: Intermediate

Materials

21 (6mm) black/silver cathedral-cut glass beads
12 (8mm) jet black Swarovski cube beads
6 (2mm) silver round beads
9 (4mm) silver spacers
2 silver crimp beads
2 (8mm) silver bead caps
3 silver spear-style head pins
2 silver kidney ear wires
Silver 3-hole lapel pin
4mm silver jump ring
2 yards ¾-inch-wide olive green satin ribbon
6 inches 24-gauge sterling silver wire
10 inches .018-inch-diameter nylon-coated flexible beading wire
12 inches olive green thread
Sewing needle
Round-nose pliers
Chain-nose pliers
Crimp pliers
Wire nippers

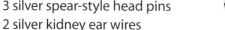

Finished Sizes

Necklace
36 inches; ties to desired length
Earrings
1¾ inches long
Pin
Approximately 4 x 1⅝ inches

Instructions

Necklace

1. Cut two 3-inch lengths of sterling silver wire. Referring to Fig. 1, use round-nose pliers to form a double loop at one end on each wire length.

2. String a crimp bead onto beading wire 1 inch from one end; place wire end through the double loop on one wire and back through the crimp bead. Use crimp pliers to flatten and fold the crimp bead.

3. Cut a 50-inch length of ribbon and tie a single knot over the crimp and double loop, leaving a 14-inch ribbon tail; position pieces so the 2½-inch straight portion of wire and 14-inch ribbon tail point in the same direction.

4. Slide a bead cap down the ribbon tail and sterling silver wire, placing it above knot. Secure bead cap by using round-nose pliers to form straight end of wire into a swirl around the ribbon and above the bead cap, leaving a hole in the middle of the swirl large enough to feed ribbon through. Adjust ribbon as needed.

5. String a black/silver cathedral-cut bead, jet black cube and a black/silver cathedral-cut bead onto beading wire; tie a knot with the ribbon onto the wire just after the beads; make the length of ribbon a bit shorter than length of beaded wire. This provides necklace with a slight curve.

6. Repeat step 5 seven additional times.

7. String a black/silver cathedral-cut bead, jet black cube, black/silver cathedral-cut bead and a crimp

Fig. 1

bead onto beading wire. Place wire end through double loop on remaining sterling silver wire from step 1 and back through the crimp bead, gently pulling wire to tighten. Flatten and fold the crimp bead. Trim excess wire.

8. Tie a single knot over the crimp and double loop, positioning wire and ribbon in the same manner as in step 3. Repeat step 4. Trim ribbon ends at an angle.

Earrings & Pin

1. Slide the following onto a head pin: silver round bead, silver spacer, jet black cube, silver spacer, black/silver cathedral-cut bead, silver spacer and a silver round bead. In the same manner as in step 1 of Necklace, use round-nose pliers to form a double loop above top bead; trim excess wire. Repeat twice.

2. Slide two of the beaded head pins onto ear wires.

3. For the pin, use a jump ring to attach remaining beaded head pin to centre hole on lapel pin. Tie a bow with remaining ribbon and hand-sew bow to the lapel pin, stitching thread through outer holes. Secure thread by tying a double knot below bow; trim excess thread. ■

Spearmint Twist

Draw bold, free-form stripes of green, turquoise and black on white ceramic rounds. Quick and easy paint pens minimize mess and maximize fun!

DESIGN BY MICHELLE MACH

Skill Level: Easy

Materials

7 (12mm) white porcelain round beads
4 (12mm) blackstone doughnut beads
4 (4mm) black onyx round beads
3 (14 x 11mm) black agate barrel beads
2 (2mm) black crimp beads
16 x 4 x 3mm silver-plated tubular add-a-bead clasp
8½ inches .019-inch-diameter nylon-coated
   flexible beading wire
Paint pens: black, aqua, turquoise, green
Crimp pliers
Wire nippers
Jewellery glue

Finished Size

8¼ inches (including clasp)

Instructions

1. Draw alternating stripes of colour with paint pens on each white bead, letting beads dry after each stripe. Outline holes on white beads with black paint pen; let dry.
2. Apply glue to bar portion of clasp and slide on a painted bead; let dry.
3. String a crimp bead ½ inch from one end of beading wire; thread short wire tail through clasp and back through crimp bead. Use crimp pliers to flatten and fold the crimp bead.
4. String a black onyx round bead, doughnut bead, painted bead, barrel bead, painted bead, doughnut bead and a painted bead.

5. String a black onyx round bead, barrel bead and a black onyx round bead. Repeat step 4, only in reverse.
6. String a crimp bead; thread wire through other half of clasp and back through crimp bead. Flatten and fold the crimp bead. Trim excess wire. ∎

SOURCE: Beads and clasp from Fire Mountain Gems and Beads.

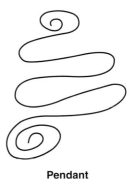

Copper Serpentine

Turquoise has been mined in the Southwest United States for hundreds of years and is believed to be a stone of life and good fortune. So go ahead, wrap and bend your way to some gorgeous good fortune!

DESIGNS BY BRENDA MORRIS JARRETT

Skill Level: Intermediate

Materials
12 (6–7mm) turquoise heishe beads
2 (6 x 10mm) red jasper tumbled rectangular beads
2 (2-inch) copper head pins
Copper wire: 49½ inches 16-gauge, 11 inches 18-gauge, 4½ inches 20-gauge, 32 inches 26-gauge
Bracelet mandrel or aluminum can 7 inches in circumference
Necklace mandrel or 16-inch-round box
Anvil
Chasing hammer or regular hammer
⁵⁄₁₆-inch wooden dowel
File
Round-nose pliers
Chain-nose pliers
Flat-nose pliers
Flush cutters

Finished Sizes
Necklace
17½ inches circumference
Bracelet
8 inches circumference
Earrings
1⅝ inches long

Instructions
Necklace Pendant
1. Cut a 9-inch length of 16-gauge copper wire and straighten it. Use round-nose pliers to form a small loop at one end. Use fingers and flat-nose pliers to form a spiral around the loop. Referring to Pendant diagram, continue to use pliers and fingers to form wire into serpentine shape. Place pendant on anvil and hammer both sides until loops are flattened.

Pendant

2. Cut a 10-inch length of 26-gauge wire. Form a small hook at one end using chain-nose pliers; attach hook to back of pendant near top of first loop; hold hook and proceed to wrap wire tightly around top of first loop, catching the hook on back underneath wrapped wire to secure it. Use flat-nose pliers to push wire wraps together.

3. String a turquoise heishe bead. Referring to photo, wrap wire tightly around top of next loop four times. String another turquoise heishe bead and wrap wire tightly around top of next loop four times. Repeat two more times, stringing turquoise

CONTINUED ON PAGE 130

heishe beads and wrapping wire around loops, referring to photo for placement. To end, wrap wire tightly around a loop four times and press wire against pendant to secure. Trim excess wire.

4. Slide a red jasper bead onto a head pin; form a wrapped head-pin loop above bead, attaching loop to bottom spiral on pendant before wrapping. Trim excess wire.

5. Cut a 3-inch length of 16-gauge wire and wrap it around the wooden dowel, forming a coil. Remove wire coil from dowel rod and cut a jump ring. Open jump ring and slide it through top spiral on pendant; close ring.

Finishing

1. Cut a 20-inch length of 16-gauge wire and file one end until it is smooth; form a small loop on opposite end and create a spiral in the same manner as for pendant. Referring to Hook diagram, hold wire with round-nose pliers ½ inch from end of spiral and pull down over one jaw of the pliers, forming a hook.

Hook

2. Wrap the wire around necklace mandrel or 16-inch-round box to set the shape. Use round-nose pliers to form an open loop ½ inch from filed end, making sure loop is perpendicular to the hook. Lightly tap both sides along length of wire with chasing hammer to harden the wire, helping it to retain its shape. Thread pendant onto wire.

Bracelet

1. Cut an 8½-inch length of 16-gauge copper wire and straighten it. Use round-nose pliers to form a small loop at one end. Use fingers and flat-nose pliers to form a spiral around the loop. Referring to Pendant diagram, continue to form wire into bracelet top piece. Place piece on anvil and hammer both sides until loops are flattened.

2. Repeat steps 2 and 3 of Pendant. Slide a red jasper bead onto a head pin; form a wrapped head-pin loop above bead, attaching loop to top spiral on bracelet piece before wrapping. Trim

excess wire. Use chain-nose pliers to carefully bend the small loop at bottom of bracelet piece so it is perpendicular to rest of piece.

3. To make cuff, cut a 9-inch length of 16-gauge wire and file one end until it is smooth; form a small loop on opposite end and create a spiral in the same manner as for pendant. Referring to Hook diagram, hold wire with round-nose pliers ½ inch from end of spiral and pull down over one jaw of the pliers, forming a hook.

4. Wrap the wire around bracelet mandrel or 7-inch aluminum can to set the shape. Use round-nose pliers to form an open loop ½ inch from filed end, making sure loop is perpendicular to the hook. Lightly tap both sides along length of wire with chasing hammer to harden the wire, helping it to retain its shape.

5. Thread the small loop end of bracelet top piece onto the hook end of cuff; close hook, trapping the piece inside the hook, forming a hinge. To fasten, hook bent end of cuff onto top spiral of hinged piece.

Earrings

1. Cut a 5½-inch length of 18-gauge wire. Use tip of round-nose pliers to form a small loop at one end. Use flat-nose pliers to form a spiral around the loop. Referring to Earring diagram, continue to use pliers and fingers to form wire into earring shape. Place piece on anvil and hammer both sides until loops are flattened.

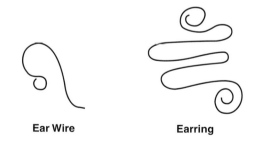

Ear Wire **Earring**

2. Cut a 6-inch length of 26-gauge wire. Form a small hook at one end with chain-nose pliers; attach hook to back of copper piece in the same manner as for necklace pendant. Following steps 2 and 3 of Pendant, attach two turquoise heishe beads to copper piece and secure wire.

CONTINUED ON PAGE 153

Disco Ball

Dazzling best describes this faceted beauty with sparkle and motion that's perfect for your New Year's Eve bash.

DESIGNS BY JEAN YATES

Skill Level: Easy

Materials
10mm Swarovski crystal rhodium-plated rhinestone balls: 3 rose, 1 crystal, 1 jet, 1 Siam, 1 erinite, 1 green tourmaline, 1 hyacinth, 1 light rose, 1 fuchsia
11 (3-inch) sterling silver 22-gauge head pins
11 (8mm) sterling silver snap-close jump rings
2 sterling silver ear posts with loops with butterfly backs
Silver rhinestone barrel clasp
2 (1½-inch) lengths sterling silver chain
12 inches sterling silver diamond-cut bead link chain
Round-nose pliers
Chain-nose pliers
Wire nippers

Finished Sizes
Necklace
14¼ inches (including clasp)
Earrings
2¼ inches long

Instructions
Necklace
1. Set aside two rose rhinestone balls to be used for earrings.

2. Slide remaining rose rhinestone ball on a head pin; use round-nose pliers to form a wrapped head-pin loop above ball. Trim excess wire. Repeat for each remaining rhinestone ball.
3. Open a jump ring and slide on rose rhinestone ball; attach jump ring to centre link of bead link chain.
4. Skip three links to the left and attach a light rose rhinestone ball in the same manner. Continue attaching the following rhinestone balls to left side of chain, skipping three links each time: Siam, crystal and hyacinth.
5. In the same manner, attach the following rhinestone balls to right side of centre link, skipping three links each time: green tourmaline, erinite, fuchsia and jet.
6. Use remaining two jump rings to attach clasp to ends of necklace.

Earrings
1. Slide a rose rhinestone ball on a head pin; form a wrapped head-pin loop above ball, attaching loop to end link of a 1½-inch chain before wrapping. Trim excess wire. Repeat once.
2. Open loops on ear posts; slide on end links of chains. Close loops. ■

SOURCES: Rhinestone balls and bead link chain from Fusion Beads; barrel clasp, sterling silver chain and ear posts from The Bead Shop; snap-close jump rings from Via Murano.

Lady in Red

Perk up your holiday wardrobe with a red beaded necklace and pendant that will look just right at all those holiday parties. Use three different colours of red for a harmonious blend of the colour of the season.

DESIGN BY CAROLE RODGERS

Skill Level: Intermediate

Materials
Red shell pendant
50 (8mm) red round beads
Silver round beads: 82 (2mm), 120 (3mm)
130 (4 x 10mm) red stick beads
24 (5mm) black pinch beads
Silver Bali-style beads: 17 (4 x 7mm), 2 (5mm)
    daisy spacers
2 (10mm) silver curved tube beads
12 (2mm) silver crimp beads
Silver Bali-style 3-strand clasp
3 (30-inch) lengths .018-inch-diameter
    nylon-coated flexible beading wire
Crimp pliers
Wire nippers
Tape

Finished Size
21½ inches (including clasp)

Instructions
1. Holding all three wires together, string a daisy spacer, curved tube, 4 x 7mm silver Bali-style bead, curved tube and a daisy spacer. Centre beads on wires. Tape one side of wires next to daisy spacer.
2. Working with one strand, string a 2mm silver round bead.

3. String a 2mm silver round bead and an 8mm red round bead; repeat four additional times. String a 2mm silver round bead and a 4 x 7mm silver Bali-style bead.
4. Repeat step 3 four additional times. String a 2mm silver round bead. Tape wire next to last bead.
5. Working with second wire on same side, string three 2mm silver round beads. String five 3mm silver round beads and a black pinch bead; repeat 11 additional times. String five 2mm silver round beads. Tape wire next to last bead.
6. Working with remaining wire on same side, string 20 red stick beads, 4 x 7mm silver Bali-style bead, 25 red stick beads, 4 x 7mm silver Bali-style bead, 20 red stick beads, 4 x 7mm silver Bali-style bead and a 2mm silver round bead. Tape wire next to last bead.
7. Loosely braid beaded strands; remove tape from outside strand and string two crimp beads. Place wire end through outside loop on one half of clasp and back through crimp beads. Gently pull wire to tighten loop; use crimp pliers to flatten and fold the crimp beads. Trim excess wire. Repeat to attach other two wires to remaining loops on clasp.
8. Remove tape from other side of necklace. Slide on pendant and attach tape to two of the wires.
9. Repeat steps 2–7 to complete remaining half of necklace. ■

SOURCES: Crimp beads and beading wire from Beadalon; pendant from Indostone.

Ice Is Nice

Ice is most definitely nice when it's frozen in this deliciously decadent, asymmetrical lariat. Wrap it around your dainty neck and prepare for maximum dazzle, darling.

DESIGN BY MARGOT POTTER

Skill Level: Easy

Materials

Swarovski crystal components: 25mm crystal snowflake, 20mm crystal shadow open square
White freshwater side-drilled oval pearls: 18 (8mm), 39 (5mm)
Crystal AB Czech glass beads:
   20 oval window, 15 flat round, 65 (5mm) faceted rondelle, 71 (8mm) teeth
18 (6mm) Swarovski crystal silver rondelles
7 (6 x 8mm) mother-of-pearl flat rectangular beads
2 sterling silver crimp ends
7mm silver-plated twisted jump ring
10mm sterling silver heavy-duty oval jump ring
5 silver star-tipped head pins
2 inches 20-gauge silver-plated craft wire
46 inches .024-inch-diameter 49-strand nylon-coated flexible bright beading wire
Round-nose pliers
2 pairs chain-nose pliers
Jumbo crimp pliers
Flush cutters

Finished Size

44½ inches

Instructions

1. Slide a 5mm pearl on a head pin; use round-nose pliers to form a wrapped head-pin loop above pearl. Trim excess wire. Repeat four additional times, three times with 5mm pearls and once with an 8mm pearl.

2. Use round-nose pliers to form a small loop at one end of craft wire; bend loop against wire at a 90-degree angle to create a bail. Slide wire through top of snowflake. The loop should be positioned centred above top of snowflake. Use round-nose pliers to form wire on front of snowflake into a small spiral. Trim excess wire and carefully flatten spiral flush to front of snowflake with fingers, being careful to not push too hard as crystal can break if too much pressure is applied.

3. Use crimp pliers to secure a crimp end to one end of beading wire by compressing wire snugly inside crimp end.

4. String all remaining beads in any pattern desired. The beading on this lariat is meant to be free-form and random.

5. After all beads have been strung, attach remaining crimp end to beading wire in the same manner as in step 3. Trim excess wire.

6. Open twisted jump ring and slide on two 5mm pearl head pins, snowflake bail and two 5mm pearl head pins; attach jump ring to one end of lariat. Close jump ring.

7. In the same manner, use heavy-duty jump ring to attach square frame and 8mm pearl head pin to other end of lariat. ■

SOURCES: Czech glass beads from York Novelty Imports Inc.; crystal rondelles from Jewelry Supply Inc.; snowflake and square frame from Swarovski North America; freshwater pearls from Fire Mountain Gems and Beads; mother-of-pearl beads from Great Craft Works; beading wire and findings from Beadalon.

Czech Polka Dots

Create a woven look without weaving a thing! Two-holed beads make this quirky cuff as easy as pie, and the earrings are the icing on the cake!

DESIGNS BY MOLLY SCHALLER

Skill Level: Intermediate

Materials
31 (8mm) 2-hole red Czech glass disc beads
194 red/gold seed beads
6 (1.3mm) gold crimp beads
2 gold jump rings
2 gold ball with loop earring posts
Gold Balls-in-a-Circle clasp
46 inches .015-inch-diameter nylon-coated
    flexible beading wire
Needle-nose pliers
Crimp pliers
Wire nippers
Tape

Finished Sizes
Bracelet
7⅜ inches (including clasp)
Earrings
1⅜ inches long

Instructions
Bracelet
1. Cut four 9-inch lengths of wire.
2. Hold two 9-inch wires together and string a crimp bead ½ inch from one end; place wire ends through a jump ring and back through the crimp bead. Use crimp pliers to flatten and fold the crimp bead.
3. With both wires together, string three seed beads.

4. Separate wires. On one wire, string seven seed beads.
5. On same wire, string one red disc followed by seven seed beads. Repeat seven additional times. Use tape to hold these beads on wire.
6. On second wire, string one seed bead, one red disc bead and one seed bead.
7. Feed wire through second hole of already strung red disc bead (Fig. 1).
8. Repeat steps 6 and 7 seven additional times. Repeat step 6 one more time.
9. Remove tape from first wire and, holding the wires together, string three seed beads and a crimp bead. Feed wire through second jump ring and back through crimp bead and a few beads. Pull to take up slack and use crimp pliers to flatten and fold the crimp bead. Trim wires.
10. Repeat steps 2–9, with second set of 9-inch wires (Fig. 2 and 3).

Earrings
1. Cut two 5-inch lengths of wire.
2. String four seed beads on one 5-inch wire, centring beads and bringing wire ends together.
3. Thread wire ends through a red disc; string a seed bead on each wire (Fig. 4). Repeat twice.
4. String a crimp bead onto the right wire; string the left wire from left to right through the crimp bead and on through the seed bead and red disc (Fig. 5). String wires in opposite directions through

the last seed bead and red disc, pulling wire ends to secure beads in place. Flatten the crimp bead with needle-nose pliers. ***Note:*** *Crimp pliers are too large to fit between the beads on these earrings.* Trim excess wire.

5. Open loop on ear wire and attach it to centre of beaded loop at top of beaded piece. Close loop.

6. Repeat steps 2–5 for a second earring. ◼

SOURCES: Clasp from HandFast; Toho seed beads and beading wire from Beadalon; Czech glass discs from Beadissimo.

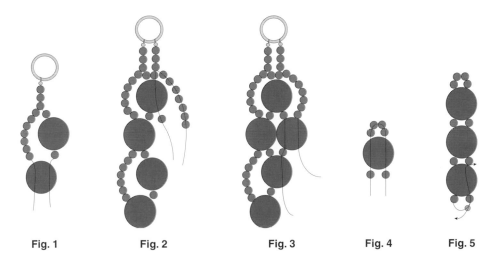

Fig. 1   Fig. 2   Fig. 3   Fig. 4   Fig. 5

Silver Spacers Bracelet & Earrings

Silver spacers never go out of style, and like potato chips, one is never enough. This bracelet made with flat disc spacer beads and embellished chain makes a delicate yet definite statement.

DESIGNS BY CAROLE RODGERS

Skill Level: Easy

Materials
2-hole silver flat disc spacers: 9 (12mm) centre hole, 10 (9.4mm) solid 20 (3 x 4mm) silver oval jump rings
5mm silver round jump ring
2 (25mm) silver kidney ear wires
Small silver lobster-claw clasp
6 inches 3.8mm silver rolo chain
Chain-nose pliers
Wire nippers

Finished Sizes
Bracelet
7¾ inches (including clasp)
Earrings
1⅞ inches long

Instructions
Bracelet
1. Open an oval jump ring and slide on a 5mm jump ring and a 9.4mm disc; close ring.

2. Cut nine pieces of chain each five links long. Set aside two pieces for earrings.
3. Open another oval jump ring and attach it to other side of 9.4mm disc from step 1; slide on a 12mm disc and one end of a 5-link piece of chain before closing jump ring.
4. Open another oval jump ring and attach it to other end of 5-link chain and other side of 12mm disc from step 3; attach ring to another 9.4mm disc before closing jump ring. The chain should be lying across the centre hole of the 12mm disc.
5. Repeat steps 3 and 4 six additional times.
6. Use an oval jump ring to attach clasp to the end of the bracelet.

Earrings
1. In the same manner as in step 3 of bracelet, use an oval jump ring to attach one piece of chain and a 12mm disc to a 9.4mm disc.
2. Attach other end of chain to opposite side of 12mm disc with an oval jump ring.
3. Slide top loop of 9.4mm disc on ear wire.
4. Repeat steps 1–3 for second earring. ■

SOURCE: Silver discs, jump rings, ear wires, clasp and chain from Beadalon.

Fancy Filigree

Layered filigree scrapbook components give this ornament antiqued elegance.

DESIGN BY TERRY RICIOLI

Skill Level: Easy

Materials

4 (1⅛ x 1⅛-inch) gold filigree squares
2 (9mm) red cabochons
10 red glass beads in assorted shapes and sizes
E beads: 4 red, 4 gold
11 gold spacers in assorted styles
4 (6mm) gold jump rings
4 (2-inch) gold head pins
Gold ear wire
Black metal art ink pad
Toothpick
Cotton swab
Heat tool (optional)
Round-nose pliers
Chain-nose pliers
Wire nippers
Jewellery glue

Finished Size

5½ inches long

Instructions

1. Place a filigree square right side facedown on worktable; use a toothpick to apply glue to square, keeping glue out of holes as much as possible. Stack another filigree square on top, right side faceup, and press together. Repeat for other two squares, adhering them together; let dry completely.

2. Use cotton swab to apply black ink to front of filigree square; wipe off excess as desired. Let dry or heat set. Repeat for back of square.

3. Glue cabochons to centre front and centre back of square; let first side dry before gluing the other. Let dry.

4. Open jump rings and attach one to each corner of filigree square.

5. Slide the following on a head pin: spacer, glass bead, spacer, two glass beads, spacer, red E bead and a gold E bead. Use round-nose pliers to form a loop above top bead; trim excess wire. Repeat once. Open loop on each and attach to opposite sides of filigree square.

6. Slide the following on a head pin: spacer, glass bead, spacer, glass bead, spacer, red E bead and gold E bead; form a loop above top bead. Trim excess wire. Open loop and attach to a jump ring on filigree square.

7. Cut off head of remaining head pin and form a loop. String the following: gold E bead, glass bead, spacer, glass bead, spacer and red E bead. Form a loop above red E bead. Trim excess wire. Open one loop and attach to remaining jump ring; open opposite loop and slide on ear wire; close loop. ■

SOURCES: Filigree squares from Cousin Corp. of America; metal ink pad from American Art Clay Co. Inc.

Artsy Abacus

Use origami paper that coordinates with your home's decor in this wall hanging with decoupaged wooden beads.

DESIGN BY MARY LYNN MALONEY

Skill Level: Easy

Materials

6 x 8-inch wooden frame

3 small eye hooks

Sawtooth hanger

7 large-hole wooden beads in assorted shapes and sizes

10 silver spacer discs (optional)

Assorted small glass and spacer beads

3 yards white chenille yarn

Metallic braids, 3 yards each colour: red, silver, gold, black

Origami printed papers

Leafing pens: gold, silver

Small block of plastic foam (optional)

Dowel rod

Flat brush

Craft drill and ⅛- and ¹⁄₁₆-inch drill bits

Floss threader

Decoupage medium

Masking tape

Finished Size

6 x 8 inches, excluding fibre tails

Instructions

1. Use a pencil to mark centre of top inside frame edge; make marks 1½ inches on each side of centre mark.

2. Using marks as guides and ¹⁄₁₆-inch drill bit, drill small pilot holes. Insert eye hooks into drilled holes and screw in place. Attach sawtooth hanger to back of frame.

3. Mark corresponding holes along inside bottom edge; use ⅛-inch drill bit to drill holes downward through to outside bottom edge.

4. Tear origami papers into small pieces. Slide a wooden bead on a dowel rod; brush decoupage medium over entire bead. Place a torn piece of paper on bead and brush decoupage medium on paper. Continue in the same manner until bead is completely covered, allowing papers to overlap. Set aside to dry. Repeat for each wooden bead. *Note: Insert dowel rod into a block of plastic foam while beads dry.*

5. Brush beads with one more coat of decoupage medium; let dry. Accent beads with leafing pens.

6. Cut all yarn and braid into three equal lengths. Gather into three bundles that contain one of each colour.

7. Tightly wrap a 1-inch piece of masking tape onto one end of a fibre bundle to provide easier threading. Insert taped end through one of the side bottom holes of frame; continue pulling fibres through until there is approximately a 6–8-inch tail below frame. Thread a wooden bead on fibres, knotting fibres at both ends of bead to secure bead in place. *Note: If bead hole is very large, string a spacer bead before and after bead.* Continue stringing a bead or two on fibres in the same manner.

8. Thread fibres through eye hook at top of frame

CONTINUED ON PAGE 152

Badge Tag Ornaments

The sky is the limit when it comes to transforming everyday household items into ornaments.

DESIGNS BY CANDIE COOPER

Skill Level: Beginner

Materials
10 (8mm) blue diamond-shaped glass beads
9 (1/0) white frost seed beads or E beads
46 (6/0) silver seed beads
Photos
Decorative papers
Plastic badge sleeves
Black permanent marker
Beaded trims: silver, red
Red rickrack
⅜-inch-wide ribbons: light blue
    velvet, red/green Christmas-
    themed
3 snowflake sequins
3 white snowflake brads
2 (1.3mm) silver crimp beads
2 light blue eyelets with
    eyelet-setting tool
10 inches .018-inch-diameter
    nylon-coated flexible
    beading wire
⅛-inch hole punch
Chain-nose pliers
Wire nippers
Multipurpose glue

Finished Size
Approximately 2½ x 4¼ inches

Getting Started
Take your photos to a store
with a colour copier to have
them reduced or enlarged to fit badge sleeves.
This is also a good way to preserve the originals.
Cut the colour copies to size and back with
decorative paper cut to fit inside badge sleeves.
Slide the paper piece into the badge sleeve.

Retro Santa
Place a line of glue along the bottom edge on the
back of the badge sleeve and adhere beaded trims;
cut off excess on edges and set aside to dry. Turn
badge sleeve over and apply lines of glue along
top and bottom edges of badge sleeve; adhere

rickrack; trim edges. Thread Christmas-themed ribbon through hole of badge sleeve and tie an overhand knot. Trim excess ribbon.

White Christmas

Cut off plastic loop on badge sleeve so that only a rectangle remains. Use a permanent marker to mark placements of eyelets in left and right corners on one long side as shown; punch holes through marks and set eyelets. Punch holes through badge tag for snowflake brads; insert brads through snowflake sequins and insert brads through holes, attaching them to tag. For hanger, string a crimp bead and seven seed beads on beading wire; insert short wire end through an eyelet and string seven more seed beads. Insert wire back through the crimp bead, forming a beaded loop. Use chain-nose pliers to flatten the crimp bead. String a blue diamond-shaped bead, seed bead, white frost bead and a seed bead; repeat until all blue diamond-shaped beads and white frost beads have been strung. String a crimp bead and seven seed beads; insert wire through other eyelet and string seven more seed beads. Insert wire back through crimp bead. Flatten the crimp bead. Trim excess wire. Tie light blue velvet ribbon around top of hanger; trim ribbon ends at an angle. ∎

SOURCE: Crimp beads and beading wire from Beadalon.

In the Bag

Transform fabric scraps, leftover beads and holiday charms into fun gift bags. Memory wire closures cinch the deal, making these wraps reusable, year after year.

DESIGN BY DIANNE DE VIENNE

Skill Level: Easy

Materials
Lightweight fabric
Assortment of small beads
Christmas-themed charms
Jump rings
Ring memory wire
Sewing machine with thread to coordinate
  with fabric
Iron
Round-nose pliers
Memory wire shears

Instructions
Bag Closure
Project note: *Memory wire is hard to cut and will damage regular wire nippers. Always use memory wire shears to cut wire coils.*
1. Cut two loops of memory wire. Use round-nose pliers to form a loop at one end of wire.
Note: *Forming loops on memory wire may take some time as it is difficult to do, due to the strength of the wire.*

2. Attach a jump ring to each charm. String beads and charms on memory wire. Form a loop at wire end.
3. To use, gather fabric at top of bag and wrap beaded wire around gathered fabric. Adjust as needed.

Fabric Bag

1. Cut a strip of fabric one inch wider than desired finished width and twice the desired finished length plus two inches. Finished sample bags measure 7 x 8½ inches and 5 x 8 inches.

2. Fold fabric strip in half with right sides facing and machine-stitch along sides ½ inch from edges. Cut fold on corners, being careful to not cut stitching. Press seams open.

3. Fold top edge down 1 inch and press; turn fabric under again so raw edge meets the fold just made. Press to create a ½-inch hem. Top-stitch hem and turn bag right side out. Press. ■

SOURCES: Charms from Gary's Arts, Crafts & Needlework Inc.; memory wire from Fire Mountain Gems and Beads.

Sparkling Snowflakes

Wire snowflake forms make these crystal window sparklers simple to put together.

DESIGNS BY MOLLY SCHALLER

Skill Level: Beginner

Materials

6 (4mm) clear Swarovski crystal bicone beads
Various colours and sizes of Swarovski crystal
    bicone and round beads
16 x 11mm baroque crystal pendant
2 (7mm) flat-back crystals
4 (3mm) silver ball memory wire end caps
2 silver cone-shaped with loop memory wire
    end caps
12 inches 20-gauge coloured copper wire
4½-inch-diameter wire snowflake form
Round-nose pliers
Chain-nose pliers
Flush cutters
Tape
Hot-glue gun
Bead cement

Finished Size

8⅛ inches long (including hanger)

Instructions

1. String a clear bicone bead on one spoke of a snowflake. String a pattern of crystals on spoke, leaving at least ⅛ inch of wire uncovered. Fold a piece of tape over end of wire. Repeat for each snowflake spoke.

2. Remove tape from one wire and trim wire so it extends approximately ⅛ inch past last bead. Apply bead cement to memory wire cone and place cone on wire, snugging it up next to last bead. Repeat for opposite spoke.

3. Repeat step 2 for each remaining spoke, attaching a ball memory wire end cap.

4. Cut a 1-inch length of wire. Use round-nose pliers to form a loop at one end of wire. String a crystal. Form another loop; trim excess wire. Open one loop and slide on baroque crystal; close loop. Open other loop and attach to one of the cone ends; close loop.

5. Form a wrapped loop at one end of remaining wire, attaching loop to opposite cone end before wrapping. Referring to photo, use pliers to form wire into a spiral hook shape for a hanger.

6. Hot-glue a flat-back crystal to centre of snowflake on each side. Let snowflake dry before hanging. ■

SOURCES: Wire snowflake form from Helby Import Co. through Fusion Beads; crystals from Swarovski North America; memory wire bead caps, wire and bead cement from Beadalon.

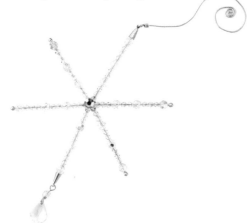

Cranberry Crush
Continued from page 119

7. Repeat step 2 to attach another wire to middle loop of clasp.

8. String a 6mm plastic, 5mm spacer, 9mm round, 5mm spacer, 3mm spacer, 6mm round, 3mm spacer, 6mm round and a 3mm spacer.

9. Insert wire through centre hole of separator bar. String a 3mm spacer, 6mm round, 3mm spacer, 8mm plastic, 3mm spacer, 5mm spacer, 10mm double crystal, 5mm spacer, 3mm spacer, 8mm plastic, 3mm spacer, 5mm spacer, 10mm round, 5mm spacer, 3mm spacer, 6mm plastic, 3mm spacer, 5mm spacer, 10mm double crystal, 5mm spacer, 3mm spacer, 8mm plastic, 3mm spacer, 6mm round and a 3mm spacer. Insert wire through centre hole of separator bar.

10. Repeat step 8, only in reverse.

11. String a crimp bead. Attach tape to wire end.

12. Repeat step 2 to attach another wire to remaining loop on slide clasp.

13. Repeat steps 3–6.

14. Check to make sure beads are snug against each other. Remove tape from one wire; thread wire end through matching loop on remaining half of clasp and back through crimp bead and several other beads. Flatten the crimp bead. Trim excess wire. Repeat for each wire.

Earrings

1. Slide the following on a head pin: 10mm double crystal, 5mm spacer and an 8mm round crystal. Use round-nose pliers to form a loop above top bead; trim excess wire.

2. Open loop on beaded head pin and attach to an eye pin; close loop. Slide a 10mm plastic round bead on eye pin; form a loop above bead. Trim excess wire. Open ear wire loop and attach eye pin; close loop.

3. Repeat steps 1 and 2 for second earring. ■

SOURCES: Plastic beads and double crystal beads from Beyond Beadery; crystal round and bicone beads from Swarovski North America; twisted crimp beads from Via Murano; toggle clasp, separator bars, slide clasp, ear wires, head pins and spacers from Rio Grande.

Artsy Abacus
Continued from page 144

and knot tightly. Trim excess fibres. Pull fibres tightly at bottom of frame and knot to secure.

9. Repeat steps 7 and 8 with remaining fibre bundles.

10. Use floss threader to string assorted small beads on fibre tails below frame; trim excess fibre as needed. ■

Porcelain Couture
Continued from page 124

end; place short wire end through bar end of toggle clasp and back through crimp bead. Use crimp pliers to flatten and fold the crimp bead.

3. String a 5mm bead cap, 9–10mm blue round bead, 5mm bead cap, cobalt blue round bead, 4mm gold round bead and a cobalt blue round bead; repeat once, only substitute a 10mm blue and white ceramic bead in place of blue round bead.

4. Repeat beading sequence in step 3, only use a 12mm ceramic bead in place of 10mm ceramic bead.

5. String a 5mm bead cap, 25mm blue and white ceramic oval bead and a 5mm bead cap. Repeat steps 3 and 4, only in reverse.

6. String a crimp bead and chain tassel; place wire end through round end of clasp and back through tassel and crimp bead. Flatten and fold the crimp bead. Trim excess wire.

Earrings

1. String a 4mm gold round bead and a cobalt blue round bead on long shank of ear wire; form a loop

below last bead. Trim excess wire.

2. Slide a 5mm bead cap, 12mm blue and white ceramic round bead and a 5mm bead cap on a head pin; form a loop above bead cap. Trim excess wire. Open loop and attach to loop on ear wire; close loop.

3. Repeat steps 1 and 2 for second earring. ■

SOURCES: Gold chain tassels and gold corrugated bead from Fire Mountain Gems and Beads; toggle clasp and beading wire from Beadalon.

Copper Serpentine
Continued from page 130

3. Repeat steps 1 and 2 to make a second earring, forming loops in the opposite direction to form a mirror image.

4. For ear wires, cut two 2¼-inch lengths of 20-gauge wire. File one end on each. Use round-nose pliers to form a small loop on the unfiled end of each. Continue to use round-nose pliers and refer to Ear Wire diagram to form ear wires. Lightly tap wires with chasing hammer to set. Open loops on ear wires and slide on copper earring pieces. ■

SOURCE: Turquoise heishe beads, red jasper beads and copper head pins from Fire Mountain Gems and Beads.

INDEX

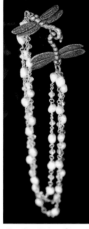

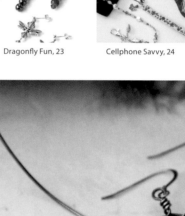

INDEX

INDEX

INDEX

Metric Equivalency Chart

MM = Millimetres   CM = Centimetres

Inches to Millimetres and Centimetres

INCHES	MM	CM	INCHES	CM	INCHES	CM
⅛	3	0.3	9	22.9	30	76.2
¼	6	0.6	10	25.4	31	78.7
⅜	10	1.0	11	27.9	32	81.3
½	13	1.3	12	30.5	33	83.8
⅝	16	1.6	13	33.0	34	86.4
¾	19	1.9	14	35.6	35	88.9
⅞	22	2.2	15	38.1	36	91.4
1	25	2.5	16	40.6	37	94.0
1¼	32	3.2	17	43.2	38	96.5
1½	38	3.8	18	45.7	39	99.1
1¾	44	4.4	19	48.3	40	101.6
2	51	5.1	20	50.8	41	104.1
2½	64	6.4	21	53.3	42	106.7
3	76	7.6	22	55.9	43	109.2
3½	89	8.9	23	58.4	44	111.8
4	102	10.2	24	61.0	45	114.3
4½	114	11.4	25	63.5	46	116.8
5	127	12.7	26	66.0	47	119.4
6	152	15.2	27	68.6	48	121.9
7	178	17.8	28	71.1	49	124.5
8	203	20.3	29	73.7	50	127.0

Our website is stuffed with all kinds of great information.

www.companyscoming.com

Save up to 75% on cookbooks.

Free recipes and cooking tips.

Free newsletter with exclusive offers.

Preview new titles.

Find older titles no longer in stores.

We're bringing the same sizzle to our Craft books as we do to our Cookbooks

More than 25 years and more than 25 million cookbooks sold—that's quite a feat.
Now we're giving you the same attention to detail in our new craft books
as we always have in our cookbooks—lots of great photos, easy-to-follow instructions
and choices galore! It's time to get a little crafty with us!

For more information and free recipes please visit us at www.companyscoming.com

Company's Coming®